4/01
2.90

4/01
2.90

# THE STORY OF
# MUSIC

# VOLUME 8

## The Music Profession

GROLIER
EDUCATIONAL

# ABOUT THIS BOOK

This book is one of a set of ten that tells the story of music from earliest times to the present day. Starting with the primitive sounds made by the crude instruments devised by early human beings, the first book traces the development of music through the centuries, describing how it evolved and how musical instruments became more refined and ever more capable of delivering beautiful sounds. The second book in the series focuses on the music of the 19th and 20th centuries, showing how the orchestra developed to become the impressively large body that it is today, and how composers ranged through a variety of musical styles, culminating in the exciting electronic experiments of the late 20th century.

Other volumes in the series look at music from around the world and U.S. music in the forms of folk, country, and Cajun, as well as gospel, blues, and jazz. A whole volume examines modern music, from rock 'n' roll to hip-hop. Another book looks at musicals, operetta, and film music, while music education and the music business are also given an entire volume. A whole book focuses on musical instruments and recording technology, while the final book in the series looks at the voice, opera, songs, and singing in general.

The books are fully illustrated, and each volume ends with a timeline, a glossary of musical terms and notation, a list of further reading, and a comprehensive index covering the complete set.

Published 2001 by Grolier Educational
Sherman Turnpike
Danbury, Connecticut 06816

© 2001 Brown Partworks Ltd

Set ISBN: 0-7172-9559-1
Volume ISBN: 0-7172-9567-2

Library of Congress Cataloging-in-Publication Data
Story of music
    p. cm.
  Includes indexes.
  Contents: v. 1. Classical music from earliest times -- v. 2. Classical music: romantic to modern -- v. 3. Music from around the world -- v. 4. Folk, country, and cajun music -- v. 5. Gospel, blues, and jazz -- v. 6. From rock and pop to hip-hop -- v. 7. Music of stage and screen -- v. 8. The music profession -- v. 9. Musical instruments and technology -- v. 10. The voice and song.
  ISBN 0-7172-9559-1 (set: alk. paper) -- ISBN 0-7172-9560-5 (v. 1: alk. paper) -- ISBN 0-7179-9561-3 (v. 2: alk. paper) -- ISBN 0-7172-9562-1 (v. 3: alk. paper) -- ISBN 0-7172-9563-X (v. 4: alk. paper) -- ISBN 0-7172-9564-8 (v. 5: alk. paper) -- ISBN 0-7172-9565-6 (v. 6: alk. paper) -- ISBN 0-7172-9566-4 (v. 7: alk. paper) -- ISBN 0-7172-9567-2 (v. 8: alk. paper) -- ISBN 0-7172-9568-0 (v. 9: alk. paper) -- ISBN 0-7172-9569-9 (v. 10: alk. paper)
  1. Music--History and criticism--Juvenile literature. [Music--History and criticism.]
  ML3928 .S76 2000
  780--dc21

                                              00-023220

For information address the publisher:
Grolier Educational, Sherman Turnpike,
Danbury, Connecticut 06816

Printed in Singapore

---

**Glossary**
Words that are explained in the glossary are printed in **bold** type the first time they appear in a chapter.

FOR BROWN PARTWORKS LTD

Editor:              Julian Flanders
Deputy editor:       Sally McFall
Design:              Evelyn Bercott
Picture research:    Brenda Clynch

Managing editor:     Lindsey Lowe
Production:          Matt Weyland

Contributor:         Terry Burrows
Consultant:          Amy Dodds

PHOTOGRAPHIC CREDITS
Front cover: Orchestra in Abbey Road Studio, London, **The Lebrecht Collection**.
Title Page: Show band on beach, **Pictor**.
**AKG London**: 6, 7, 8; **Arena**: 21, 24tr, 26, 57; **Artemis Music Ltd**: 54; **AMS**: 61; **Image Bank**: Archive Photos 10bl, 48; **Duncan Brown**: 53; **Brown Partworks**: 36tr; **Corbis**: Nubar Alexanian 13, James L Amos 25, Karen Mason Blair 5tl, Kevin Fleming 17, Ruen Hellestad 32tr, Kim Sayer 62, Ted Spiegel 5; **Julian Flanders**: 39; **Hulton-Getty**: 30, 33; **The Lebrecht Collection**: 9cl & tr, 10tr, 20, 34, 42, 46tl & br, 58, David Farrell 15br, Jim Four 14, 12, 24bl, Dave G. Houser 40, S Lauterwasser 19, Nigel Luckhurst 4, Matthew Mendleson 41tl, Wladimir Pollack 16, Neal Preston 38, S.I.N 28, Nicky J Sims, 42, 44, UPI 35, 36br; **Mosaic Images**: Francis Wolff 49br; **Peter Newark**: 11; **Philips Consumer Electronics**: 67br; **Pictor**: 22, 66; **Pictorial Press**: 18, 31, 55; **Popperfoto**: 50bl; **Sound Technology plc**: 60; **Sylvia Pitcher Picture Library**: 47; **Redferns**: Robin Little 32bl, Robert Knight 23, Michael Ochs Archives 56, David Redfern 65, Jon Wilton 29; **Retna**: Chris Taylor 41br; **Rex Features**: *The Times* 67t, Edward Webb 45; **S.I.N.**: 28; **Whitfield Street Recording Studio**: 52; **David Swanson**: Curtis Institute of Music 15tr; **Yamaha-Kemble Music**: 64.
Page 37 courtesy EMI Records Ltd, page 49bl courtesy Blue Note Records.
**Key**: b=below, t=top, c=center, l=left, r=right.
Every effort has been made to trace copyright holders and gain permission for material reproduced in this volume. We regret if any errors have occurred.

Artworks: Mark Walker
Musical notation: Harry Boteler

# Contents

## VOLUME 8
## The Music Profession

# CHAPTER 1

# Music Theories and Education

From the great philosophers of ancient Greece to the most innovative music educators of today, people have always communicated their ideas about music to others. This has inspired many to make music part of their daily lives.

From the large number of ancient Greek documents that refer to music, it is clear that this art played a vital role in the daily lives of Greek people. The documents also prove that the ancient Greeks had a system of music **notation**, even if the few surviving fragments of it leave no clues as to its meaning. It is therefore difficult to imagine what the music of ancient Greece really sounded like. Yet the documents do reveal that many Greeks, including the philosopher Socrates, practiced the art of music.

**Above: Shinichi Suzuki directs a group of violin students. He created his own method of teaching music that is still used today.**

In fact, the ancient Greeks laid the foundations for the future study and enjoyment of music.

## Music as math

The ancient Greeks first saw music as a phenomenon to be analyzed rather than as an art to be appreciated. The philosopher Pythagoras viewed music as a branch of mathematics (see Volume 1, page 10). He and his followers were the first to understand the relationship between the **pitch** of a note and the length of the string that produced it. The Pythagoreans showed that its pitch depended on the way in which the string vibrated. These discoveries led to the science of **acoustics**, which is still studied today.

## Music as a moral influence

Music was also at the heart of the teachings of Plato (428–348 B.C.). He believed in the emotional and moral power of scales and made links between people's characters and the music they listened to. The scales that he thought helped restore order to

**Above: Aristotle and Plato (left) in *The School of Athens*—a painting by Raphael.**

**Greek Phrygian Scale**

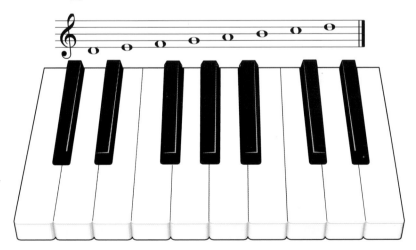

**Above: The Greek Phrygian scale can be played on the white notes of the keyboard from D to D. In medieval times the Greek scale names were used to create modes. Yet through a strange misunderstanding the Greek Phrygian scale became the Dorian mode, and what is now called the Phrygian mode goes from E to E (see Volume 3, page 6).**

the soul were the Phrygian, which portrayed the moderate person who was well off, and the Dorian, which portrayed the brave person under stress. He declared that rhythms and melodies must be especially chosen for their effect on people, since they sank deep into the soul and remained there, and the wrong music could be emotionally and morally damaging.

Plato believed that music should be simple, since complex rhythms and melodies led to depression and disorder. He thought that instruments and voices should sound in **unison** and that solo instrumental performances were nothing more than meaningless **virtuosity**. Plato also believed that the words sung by the singers were more important than the music that accompanied it.

Following the ideas of Plato, Aristotle (384–322 B.C.) also believed that music had the power to mold human character. However, he saw the influence of music in a more positive light, advocating a rich, if disciplined, musical diet.

### Music that makes sense

One of Aristotle's pupils, Aristoxenus, encouraged a step back from the Pythagorean notion of music as a science. Aristoxenus thought music had a functional role that needed to be judged not by mathematical ratios but simply by listening. Considered the first practical music theorist, he taught that individual notes should be understood in their relation to one another in order for music to make sense (see Volume 1, pages 10–11).

### Early Christian ideas on music

The view of Plato and Aristotle—that music had an effect on people's moral character—greatly influenced the Christian church over 1,000 years

later. In the Middle Ages Christianity was vital in the spread of music education throughout Europe. Like Plato, the Christian church also believed that the singers' words were the most important element of the music and that melody and rhythm—whether supplied by voices or by the organ or the few instruments accepted in the Christian church—should only serve as a background to highlight the sacred text (see Volume 1, pages 13–15). This emphasis on the words can be heard in examples of monastic **plainsong** that still exist.

St. Augustine (354–430), the greatest thinker of early Christianity, was attracted to music and could see its benefits as a part of worship. In *De Musica*, his book on music, he wrote that the study of music theory led to spiritual contemplation. Yet, like Plato, he feared the potential danger

Right: Vittore Carpaccio's painting *The Vision of St. Augustine,* from the 16th century, shows the saint at work in his study.

of music's emotional power. Thomas Aquinas (1224–1274), who embraced St. Augustine's thinking some 900 years later, returned to the view of music as mathematical, reflecting the movement of the heavens and the overall order of things on earth.

## Medieval Christian education

The earliest universities in medieval Europe taught a formal Christian education, based on the Platonic view of music adopted by the Christian church. Music formed one of the seven liberal arts, which were divided into the "quadrivium" (geometry, arithmetic, astronomy, music) and the "trivium" (grammar, rhetoric, logic). The church believed that although the liberal arts were not necessary in order to worship God, they were important if a student was to truly understand the scope of God's power. This educational process led to the sophisticated appreciation of music as an art form among educated people.

## Music for the emotions

The Swiss philosopher Jean-Jacques Rousseau (1712–1778) was one of the most influential figures in the development of education in the 17th century. His work marked the birth of the Romantic period, in which feelings were considered superior to reason. His work revolutionized how

---

## *Jean-Jacques Rousseau had a major effect on the way children were educated*

---

the arts, particularly music, were appreciated, and had a major effect on the way children were educated.

In his book *A Discourse on Equality* Rousseau describes the

development of the human race and makes a distinction between man as formed by nature ("natural man") and man as shaped by society and by his education and appreciation of the arts ("social man"). Good education, he argued, should develop the nature, or essence, of man. He thought that the most important element in music was song, which he described as primitive man's original cry of passion. He insisted that all music should be based on song and should appeal primarily to the emotions and not to the intellect.

Rousseau's major work on education, *Émile*, describes the education of a young boy in a world inhabited only by the child and his tutor, free from the influence of

**Above: The French author, philosopher, and educationalist Jean-Jacques Rousseau as he appears in Allan Ramsey's *Portrait in Armenian Costume*, painted in 1766.**

"social man." Rousseau shows how a natural education away from the influence of society enabled Émile to become social, moral, and rational, while retaining his true nature.

### Educating children
Rousseau's *Émile* had a strong effect on Swiss educational reformer Johann Heinrich Pestalozzi (1746–1827) in the next century. He insisted on education for the poor and stressed teaching methods that strengthened the student's own natural abilities. Pestalozzi felt that children's natural abilities developed better when they participated in a group, and he taught singing, drawing, writing, and physical exercise as group activities.

**Below: Swiss educational and social reformer Johann Heinrich Pestalozzi believed that the poor should be educated. He also believed that children developed more quickly when they took part in group activities.**

Pestalozzi's methods became widely accepted, and most of his principles are now a fundamental part of mainstream elementary school education. He encouraged the teaching of music to children at an early age and was a big influence on many of the most common methods of childhood music teaching used in the 20th century, such as those developed by Émile Jaques-Dalcroze, Carl Orff, and Zoltán Kodály.

## *Pestalozzi encouraged music education to be introduced to children at an early age*

The German Carl Orff (1870–1942)—famous as the composer of the exhilarating **choral cantata** *Carmina Burana*—also developed a system of teaching music to children through group performances and exercises based on eurythmics (see box on right). He encouraged students to **improvise** on eurythmic movements by adding various percussion instruments, particularly xylophones and the metallophones used in gamelan music (see Volume 3, page 50). Orff set out to prove that all children were musical and, with the right training through group improvisation, could develop a sense of rhythm, pitch, and musical form.

A more recent approach to music teaching was developed by the Japanese violinist Shinichi Suzuki (1898–1998). His system is based on the idea that children learn music in much the same way that they learn their first language—by being constantly surrounded by it, listening, watching, hearing sounds repeated, and receiving encouragement from those around them.

# EURYTHMICS

In the early 1900s the Swiss composer Émile Jaques-Dalcroze (1865–1950) created a system called "eurythmics" to develop people's awareness of musical rhythm. He applied this system to elementary school children, teaching them to make movements with their bodies as a way of representing rhythms. His aim was to make the current of communication between a person's brain and body stronger and quicker, thereby heightening their sense of rhythm. Pupils were taught how to indicate musical notes by movements of their feet and body, and rhythmic beats by movements of their arms.

His success with volunteer school classes led to an invitation to start his own eurythmics institute in a suburb of Dresden, Germany, in 1910. He visited England with some students to give lectures and demonstrations in 1912,

**Above: Émile Jaques-Dalcroze**

which resulted in the founding of the London School of Dalcroze Eurythmics in 1913. When World War I broke out in 1914, he returned to Switzerland and started the Institut Jaques-Dalcroze in Geneva. Afterward, similar schools emerged in Berlin, Vienna, Paris, Stockholm, and New York. Although eurythmics is no longer fashionable today, Jaques-Dalcroze's ideas have generated a more creative approach to musical education for children.

**Above: Students perform a dance using the movements of eurythmics.**

Whichever teaching system is used, modern research has shown beyond any doubt that music can play a vital role in children's development. In addition to the value of learning music for its own sake, other areas of a child's learning—such as movement, speech, and listening patterns—can be improved by early musical training.

## Music education in the U.S.

In the U.S. education in general, not just in music, was strongly influenced by the followers of Pestalozzi. In the 1800s there was a growing interest in methods of education—particularly in the Northeast—which prompted a wide and steady movement toward a standardized public education. Most of these educational innovations were based around the city of Boston and eventually gained a hold throughout the rest of the country.

The first great music educator in the U.S. was Reverend William Channing Woodbridge (1749–1845). During a trip to Europe to recover from an illness, he met Pestalozzi. On returning to the U.S., Woodbridge became an active crusader for

Pestalozzi's principles and for the development of music education in general. Although he met with much resistance from the educational establishment of the time, one man—Lowell Mason—came to embrace and expand these techniques.

## America's great music educator

Lowell Mason (1792–1872) was a self-taught musician who succeeded in mastering a large number of instruments, in addition to being an accomplished composer and choir director. Yet his ultimate dream was to have his pioneering ideas of musical education taught in the growing U.S. public school system. He published an influential series of 61 articles in the *New York Musical Review*, which ran under the title "Pestalozzian Music Teaching." Mason held music classes wherever he could, teaching people in his own home until a formal music

Above: Lowell Mason was the main crusader for music to be taught in U.S. public schools.

# THE KODÁLY METHOD

Above: Zoltán Kodály at the piano.

The Hungarian composer and music educator Zoltán Kodály (see Volume 2, pages 43–44) inspired a revolution in the teaching of music that spread around the world. The "Kodály Method" is based around five principles: music is a prime necessity of life; only music of the highest quality is good enough for children; music education must begin nine months before the child's birth; instruction in music must be a part of everyone's general education; and the ear, the eye, the hand, and the heart must all be trained together. According to Kodály, children's natural means of musical expression is the voice, so music instruction should be vocally based. Children are taught to sing in tune, to improvise, and to "**sight-sing**" through singing games. His approach concentrated on teaching children their own national folk music, which he believed eventually led to the understanding and appreciation of the music of all styles and cultures.

school was created. He was dedicated to the teaching of music to ordinary people and, most importantly, showed that all children were capable of learning music.

Mason overcame much resistance from educational policy-makers by showing that not only did music help with student discipline by teaching them a subject they enjoyed, but it could also further their understanding and involvement in religion through the study and practice of sacred music. This last point formed a persuasive argument in the staunchly religious climate of 19th-century America. Yet teaching music in public schools was still some time away.

One of Mason's greatest dreams was fulfilled in 1833, when he founded the Boston Academy of

Music—America's first dedicated music school. Mason himself was the principal teacher and organized all the courses and classes, gearing the goals of the academy to mirror his own personal aims. Boston Academy of Music became well known during the 1840s, developing the very first school of instrumental music and holding the first regular orchestral concerts in the country. Its symphony orchestra would outlive the Academy itself, becoming immensely successful with audiences and pioneering many new compositions of the time—it gave the first U.S. performances of the first, second, and fifth symphonies by Ludwig van Beethoven.

Mason began teaching in the Boston Public School in 1838 under a resolution passed by the school committee. He also gave independent classes and lectures, and published many articles. By 1900 music had found its way in some form into most U.S. public schools, for which Mason was almost solely responsible.

## Concert and marching bands

The development of instrumental music education in the U.S. coincided with the rise of concert and marching bands. This was partly due to the large influx of immigrants from European communities who brought their music and instruments with them. In Europe, however, music education in schools was only the privilege of the upper classes, whereas Lowell Mason's efforts firmly directed such an education toward the general public. Because of this, by the early 1900s those immigrants who might not have had the opportunity to learn a musical instrument in their former countries had little problem in finding a music teacher or band within their local U.S. communities.

The emergence of **professional** symphony orchestras in the larger U.S. cities also helped further music education. Modeled on European orchestras, most of them were founded in the late 19th century, generally in the American Northeast.

**Left: John Philip Sousa was America's most famous composer and leader of marching bands.**

# SOUSA ON THE MARCH

John Philip Sousa (1854–1932) and his band were the first commercially successful instrumental group in the United States. Sousa's parents were both immigrants: his father was born in Spain, of Portuguese parents, and his mother in Bavaria. He joined the U.S. Marine Band as a trombonist in 1868 and later played in theater orchestras as a violinist before returning to the U.S. Marine Band as its conductor. In 1892 he started his own band, which performed widely throughout the country and was overwhelmingly responsible for the rise in popularity of the community band. By the end of the 19th century there were well over 10,000 marching bands in the U.S., and the music for Sousa's famous **marches** had been sold to nearly a quarter of them. While turning the concert band into a finely tuned and elegant musical ensemble, Sousa carved a path for instrumental music's first well-known virtuosos: cornet soloists Joseph Arban (1825–1889) and Herbert L. Clarke (1867–1945) set standards of playing that are considered benchmarks to this day.

Right: Students at the Juilliard School of Music in New York City playing in the orchestra at the school.

Classical instrumental music grew in popularity, and the concert band became the perfect vehicle for music in schools. School administrators realized that concert bands could also serve as vehicles for school spirit and unity, through marching in parades and playing for sporting events and other school and community events. The marching band's role developed over the years, combining slick **choreography** with military-style uniforms. These bands typically provided half-time entertainment at high-school football games.

By the 1960s most high-school music programs generally included some form of choir, a concert band, a marching band, and, in some cases, a jazz-oriented "big band."

## Music conservatories

After Lowell Mason's Academy of Music, other formal music schools began to appear in Boston in the late 19th century. Modeled directly on European conservatories, the music was also usually European classical in nature. The first of these were the

Boston Conservatory and the New England Conservatory, both founded in 1867. Others appeared afterward that provided a similar education. In the Mason tradition they boasted small classes, individual training, and were geared toward the general population, not just the wealthy. Until the early 1900s such music classes tended to be free of charge.

Music conservatories still exist in much the same manner, but they are generally more focused on producing virtuoso instrumental performers. Among the most noted of these institutions are the Juilliard School of Music in New York, the Manhattan School of Music, the New England Conservatory, and the San Francisco Conservatory. The largest music school for performance in the U.S. is the University of Indiana, which is sometimes humorously referred to as the "note factory." At the other end of the scale is the Curtis Institute of Music in Philadelphia—a small but top-notch establishment with only one orchestra. It is widely believed to be the toughest orchestral school in which to win a place and is geared exclusively toward orchestra and chamber music performance. Music conservatories also grant degrees in composition, but they are, like many BA degrees, of little value in the job world unless the student goes on to graduate school for a PhD or DMA (Doctor of Musical Arts) degree.

Full jazz programs are now almost as common as classical study in these institutions. Schools like the New England Conservatory and Berklee College of Music in Boston have gained fine reputations for providing rigorous technical training for jazz musicians. Similarly, Juilliard has seen such notable jazz stars as trumpet virtuosos Miles Davis and Wynton Marsalis pass through its doors.

### College and university courses

The main difference between music education in colleges and universities and that of conservatories is that the first two tend to concentrate more on theoretical study than on music

---

## One field of music that has grown rapidly in recent years is music technology

---

performance. Universities and colleges usually offer a wider choice of courses, and music majors can also take other courses unrelated to music. Such institutions also focus more on the appreciation of music rather than practical performance, similar to the difference between that of studying literature or creative writing. Colleges and universities can also offer advanced degrees and doctorates in music education, composition, music history, ethnic music history, music therapy, and conducting.

One field of music that has grown rapidly in recent years is music technology. The ever-changing world of **digital music** has made the subject increasingly popular. The Berklee College of Music, one of the more forward-thinking music institutes, has outstanding studio facilities and is well known for creating technology specialists. Famous for its jazz courses, Berklee now also gives instruction in commercial, pop, and rock music. This is undoubtedly a direction an increasing number of music schools will take in the future.

# MODERN METHODS

Wynton Marsalis (b. 1961), one of the most celebrated trumpet players in jazz and classical music since the 1980s, has also made a name for himself in the field of music education. Marsalis is devoted to teaching young people how to understand the basic elements of music and appreciate different styles of music. He does this by comparing music to things that children can relate to. For example, rhythmic structures are compared to a basketball or football game, and the sonata form (see Volume 1, page 53) is explained by a story about chasing a pet hamster through a shopping mall. He uses visual aids like models and props to bring musical ideas to life, such as bouncing a basketball to count out rhythmic beats and putting up models of skyscrapers to show the musical form of 12-bar blues (see Volume 5, page 21). Marsalis's aim is to make learning about music fun. His enthusiastic and imaginative teaching methods can be experienced in the lectures and workshops he gives at New York's Lincoln Center, where he is the Artistic Director of Jazz, as well as in the video and book *Marsalis on Music* (1995).

**Below: Wynton Marsalis makes learning music fun for children.**

# CHAPTER 2

# Careers in Music

Whether one dreams of becoming an opera singer or rock star, or one is drawn to teaching or music therapy, the best reason to choose a music career is for the sheer love of it, since plenty of motivation and hard work will be required.

Having a successful career in music requires more than simply being a good musician. From playing in a classical orchestra to sitting in on a recording session with a rock band, the most important character trait is the ability to "**network**" with the right people and to advertise your skills to the full. Just as in many areas of life, the key to success is often likely to be the result of motivation and self-belief rather than ability.

### The life of a musician

Being a **professional** performer in any style of music is one of the most unpredictable careers a person can choose. Those working at the top of their professions can be among the world's biggest earners, yet for most it is likely to mean insecurity, irregular work, unsociable hours, and an endless search for the next paycheck.

For the stability-conscious musician a **semiprofessional** or **amateur** career

**Above:** The orchestra of London's Royal Academy of Music performing at the Duke Hall, conducted by Tadaaki Otaka.

may be more suitable. An example of this is that of the traditional bar band (a band that regularly plays in bars in the evenings and on weekends) whose members hold down day jobs during the week. Some musicians provide themselves with a safety net by acquiring a fallback career. It will either be work they can do from time to time when they are unable to make a living from music or a career they can go back to should their music career come to an end. Although this is a sensible approach, dividing the time between two careers can create built-in frustration, especially on those occasions when one interferes with the other. Few have managed to walk this tightrope with any real success.

The starting points and career paths for professional musicians can vary immensely depending on the type of music the musician wants to play. A career in classical music is one of the most straightforward, yet competitive, paths to pursue.

**Above: A student arriving for his cello class at the prestigious Curtis Institute of Music in Philadelphia.**

### Classical orchestras

Becoming a member of a top symphony orchestra is very difficult. Any instrumentalist who succeeds will have been formally trained to the highest standard, usually the result of years of study with the best teachers

## CLASSICAL SOLO STARS

The career of a classical music soloist on any instrument is difficult to predict. **Virtuoso** musicians—those whose technical skills and abilities to interpret any musical work surpass even those who have been trained to the highest level—are a great rarity.

Sir Yehudi Menuhin (1916–1999) was perhaps the greatest violin virtuoso of the 20th century. He studied the instrument from the age of four, and by the age of eight he had already stunned the music world with his interpretation of Mendelssohn's notoriously difficult Violin Concerto. From the age of 12 he was an established player in the classical arena.

Although Menuhin's career is an extraordinary example, most classical music virtuosos are identified by their early teens. Such musicians

**Above: Yehudi Menuhin playing at the Bath Festival in England during the 1960s.**

have a special quality in their playing that is difficult to define but is often referred to as "genius." No amount of training or practice can ever hope to create this quality in a musician's playing if it is not there to be discovered and nurtured in the first place.

# AUDITIONING FOR A SYMPHONY ORCHESTRA

**Above: The Rotterdam Philharmonic Orchestra from the Netherlands performing under the conductor Riccardo Chailly.**

Auditions for symphony orchestras follow a very formal procedure. Candidates are generally asked to perform behind a screen, out of view of the judges, who are usually the conductor and senior members of the orchestra. Often the candidates are identified only by a number to make the selection process completely unbiased. This way, judgments are based entirely on the candidate's musical performance. The applicants are usually expected to play exactly the same music, chosen from the standard orchestral **repertoire**, which they will have studied and perfected for years.

In the most famous ensembles—such as the Boston Philharmonic or Berlin Symphony orchestras—salaries can be high, since they include some of the world's finest musicians. Indeed, such are the high standards in these orchestras that vacancies may remain unfilled even after as many as 400 to 500 auditions have taken place.

at the finest music schools and conservatories (see pages 12–13). Only this type of education can prepare musicians for the grueling auditions at which they will have to compete with hundreds of other musicians for a place in an orchestra.

The procedures for advertising and filling vacancies for top orchestras are tightly controlled by the Musicians' Union. When a seat, or position, becomes available in a professional symphony orchestra, a formal job announcement goes out nationwide. The orchestra's administrator may expect to receive at least 200 to 300 applications for one position.

Considering that no more than a dozen orchestras in the U.S. offer a full-time salary, this is not surprising.

## Making it as a professional

Playing professionally in other formal classical setups takes luck, hard work, and a growing book of contacts. A basic requirement is to be a top-notch instrumentalist and **sight-reader**. An ability to play a second instrument is also useful, as is the ability to play with a group and to prepare and learn material before rehearsals.

There are many professional chamber music ensembles, such as brass quintets, string quartets, and woodwind quartets. Most hold professional residencies—meaning that they have an agreement to play somewhere on a regular long-term basis—at colleges and universities, as well as going on tours and making commercial recordings. Very few entirely professional chamber music ensembles exist without the support of an educational institution.

U.S. military bands also offer a full-time salary to their musicians. Yet unlike symphony orchestras, which are tied to a single location for much of the time, military bands tour widely, often playing in parades and at holiday functions.

## Conducting an orchestra

Being the conductor of a professional orchestra is often viewed as the artistic peak of the classical music world. If jobs in a symphony orchestra are hard to come by, then those for conductors are like gold dust. The conductor is the orchestra's artistic leader. The public sees the glamorous side of the conductor's job, standing before the musicians on a **podium**, controlling the beats, **tempo**, and dynamics of the music with a wave of the hands, or baton. Yet it is behind the scenes that the most important work is done.

A conductor is largely responsible for selecting the music the orchestra will play. Therefore, the ability to balance artistic vision with the commercial demands of the paying public is essential.

**Below: The marching band of the Citadel Corps of Cadets in Charleston, South Carolina, strut their stuff during a military parade.**

The conductor also acts as the figurehead of the orchestra. Indeed, in the top ensembles the conductor will be among the best-known and well-respected names in the music world—people who have earned the title "maestro" from their colleagues and peers. In the past century characters like Arturo Toscanini (1867–1957) created the model for the modern conductor by combining outstanding skills as a musician with a control over his musicians that bordered on the obsessive. Conductors like Sir Georg Solti (1912–1997) and Herbert von Karajan (1908–1989) followed in his wake. Other maestros, like Leonard Bernstein (1918–1990), have also become famous as composers.

## The making of a maestro

The job of conductor requires incredible skill and knowledge as a musician, the sort that comes from many years of formal training. This often takes place under the guidance of the finest tutors in the world's top conservatories. When a conductor takes on a piece of music, he or she has to have a total understanding of every note on the **score** and how it should be played.

Conductors must also have the complete respect of their orchestras so that their musicians trust in their artistic vision. This means that successful conductors must possess

---

### The job of conductor requires incredible skill and knowledge as a musician

---

excellent leadership skills to get the best out of their musicians.

Becoming a "maestro" is not for the impatient: few make the grade until they are in their forties. In addition, they must have a flair for self-promotion and a keen awareness of their relationship to the concert-going public. The conductor has traditionally been a male profession, yet the past 50 years have seen an increasing number of females taking to the podium, most notably the U.S. conductor Sarah Caldwell (b. 1924).

## Conductor training grounds

Those with ambitions to be a conductor will either have trained as classical musicians or composers and probably have made a name for themselves at one of the major conservatories. Graduate degrees are necessary, as well as undergoing a number of residencies and festival internships—periods during which a conductor conducts an orchestra under the supervision of a more experienced conductor—such as those offered at the Pierre Monteux

Below: The great conductor Arturo Toscanini discusses the interpretation of a piece of music with Alexander Hilsberg, the leader and first violinist of the Philadelphia Orchestra—a top U.S. symphony orchestra.

Left: The flamboyant composer and maestro Leonard Bernstein, baton in hand, shows the presence and dramatic flair that a top conductor needs to possess.

conducting school in Maine. Most conductors rise through the ranks by finding posts or "mentorships" assisting established conductors. Since Europe is still viewed as the true home of classical music, study in Europe can only improve an already impressive set of musical credentials.

Of course, conductors can work at many different levels. For example, many music teachers need to have the ability to conduct their school or college orchestras, and the same basic conducting skills apply here as for the most high-profile orchestras, although perhaps at a less developed or highly specialized level. Conductors are also needed for operas, musicals, ballets, choirs, **choruses**, and jazz ensembles.

## Singing careers

Without a doubt the most exacting career for any singer is that of the opera singer. Not only must the voice be trained to a physically demanding level, but dramatic skills are also needed in order to perform on stage convincingly. The vocal training for opera singers is long and grueling. Beginning with both undergraduate and graduate degrees in music, vocal coaching continues throughout their professional careers. Indeed, opera singers are usually well into their thirties before their voices have matured. Of the many that train to this level, few achieve success on the "opera circuit"—the great opera houses of the U.S. and those of Paris, London, and Milan. Singers who fail to make the top grade often turn to teaching in academies or to individual voice coaching. Others turn to the less exacting but potentially high-earning world of Broadway musicals.

On a less formal level many fine vocalists take up careers as backing singers, where they back up other

Above: The singers Dmitri Hvorostovsky, as Francesco, and Paula Delligatti, as Amalia, displaying some of the acting skills necessary for opera. This is a scene from the opera *I masnadieri* by Giuseppe Verdi.

singers or musicians on recordings, **jingles** (music used in advertising), TV commercials, or in live performance. These jobs may be full time or **freelance**—without a long-term commitment to any one organization—and can involve much travel if the singer is working as part of a touring band or ensemble. The main responsibility of the vocalist is to learn the parts he or she will be singing and to attend rehearsals. Backing vocalists should be versatile and flexible; those performing on recordings, jingles, TV, and radio will also need to read music well and to catch on quickly, making a minimum of errors. The abilities to **improvise** and sing harmony are also greatly prized—especially if the singer can create additional vocal lines without the need for a music **arranger**.

## The jazz world

Jazz is probably the most difficult musical area in which to find paid performance work, since—in spite of booms like the jazz age and the big-band era of the 1920s and 1930s—it does not have much of a mainstream following. Therefore, only the major names make large amounts of money. In fact, many musicians who are known and respected by jazz fans may be struggling to make a good living out of playing.

Most jazz musicians start out by playing a number of low-paid jobs in the hope of getting a name and an audience. To do this it is generally necessary to set up base in a major city: in the U.S. New York City is largely recognized as the center of the jazz world, although Los Angeles also has an important jazz scene. On the European side Paris also attracts jazz musicians—a devoted audience and support for jazz have existed in the French capital since the 1920s (see Volume 5, page 49). Once set up, a jazz musician's success often depends on gaining the respect of other jazz musicians, since opportunities to play will increase from invitations to "sit in" at **gigs** with various jazz ensembles that already have regular bookings.

Most professional jazz musicians cannot survive off performance alone, and even the most famous cannot live off performing only in the U.S., so long periods are often spent playing in Europe and the Far East. For some reason jazz is less appreciated by the ordinary concert-going public in its founding country than almost anywhere else in the world.

Aside from the uncertain world of performance, other opportunities for jazz musicians to earn an income do exist elsewhere. As jazz has become more respected over the past 50 years, it has gained respect in the academic world. Recognized as an extremely important part of African-American history and the only major music style to have truly originated in the U.S., jazz has found a new home in many U.S. universities and conservatories. This has helped it survive and thrive away from the pressures of the commercial music world.

## Paths to pop stardom

There is no surefire way to make it in commercial music. No matter the style or quality of the music, success is most likely to depend on image, presentation, and marketing. Making it as a pop artist or part of a group takes extreme motivation as well as incredible luck. Of the thousands of bands that exist in every major city, only a handful will ever manage to get a recording contract of any kind.

Although some people might not consider popular music to be a serious art form, many rock and pop artists take themselves very seriously indeed. This can lead to a conflict of interests when the artist realizes that to become a major act requires a sum of money for marketing and advertising that can run into millions of dollars. People or organizations investing in such acts may therefore be less interested in the "artistic" quality of the product than in its money-making potential. This can place great pressures on the artists to adapt their

**Left: Members of drummer Art Blakey's Jazz Messengers in 1985: (left to right) Timothy Williams (trombone), Jean Toussaint (tenor saxophone), Terence Blanchard (trumpet), and Donald "Duck" Harrison (alto saxophone). Blakey always recruited excellent young musicians from U.S. universities and colleges for his bands. Many have gone on to become well-known names in the jazz world.**

21

work to the marketplace. This can be a demeaning prospect for those who wish to succeed on their talent alone.

## Function bands

Without a record deal or a heavy schedule of live performances there is little way of making a reasonable living out of playing commercial pop and rock music. If a musician's main objective is to play in a rock or pop band, and financial security is a big issue, a "function band" could be the answer. These groups usually have a widely varying repertoire, which allows them to perform for almost any event—from weddings, bar mitzvahs, and private parties to corporate functions and dance clubs.

A good all-round function band covers material by well-known recording artists of different musical styles, adapting its repertoire to suit the clients' demands. Many of these gigs can be formal-dress occasions, so tuxedos or suits for men, or long

**Below: A function band at a beach hotel in Miami. They are wearing the typical function-band costume of formal waistcoats and ties.**

gowns for women, may be necessary. The work is usually well paid, as well as being rewarding in terms of performance experience and the development of instrumental skills. However, the lack of originality the musician is expected to bring to the material, and the public disinterest during such gigs, can be discouraging, if not soul-destroying.

Floor-show bands are another option. They work on a similar basis, yet perform in cabarets, nightclubs,

---

### *For musicians seeking financial security, a function band could be the answer*

---

hotels, resorts, cruise ships, cafés, and bars. However, unlike the function groups whose job is simply to provide the music, floor-show bands are expected to actively entertain their audience. Therefore a good deal of planning and rehearsal is necessary, and the musicians should feel fairly comfortable actively engaging with their audiences. Floor-show groups travel frequently, often playing in one location for several weeks before moving on to the next.

## Session musicians

Also known as freelance musicians, studio musicians, session players, or backup musicians, session musicians "play to order"—in the manner that the band leader or session producer directs them—in the recording studio or for live performance.

In addition to being a good musician, the session player has to be reliable, responsible, and easy to get along with. The best session players are capable of performing in a wide variety of styles. Some also find that

they can get more work by being able to play a number of instruments. Depending on the type of music being played, it may also be important to know how to sight-read.

A session musician's career takes time to develop, since it depends on building a solid reputation for both musicianship and personality. It can be exciting and varied, but to begin with the musician will often live from hand to mouth with no real guarantee of steady work in the future, no health insurance, and no retirement plan. If successful, however, it can be highly rewarding financially: playing on rock and pop albums, top L.A. session players have been known to earn as much as the artists themselves. If they strike it lucky, they can receive a large check every year for many years on recordings made in the past.

Session players may work on film and TV music, **records**, **demos**, or jingles. They are usually hired by a record company, producer, or band and paid an hourly fee set by the Musicians' Union. Since these activities usually take place in major cities, most of the top session names

are based in New York or Los Angeles, although there are also growing film and studio cultures in Seattle, Salt Lake City, and Toronto.

## Playing film music

Among the best-paid freelance work is playing film music. All musicians who

**Above: Guitarist Steve Lukather is one of L.A.'s top session musicians. He is also a member of a band called Toto, made up of other L.A. session musicians. Toto has made its own albums and provided the background music for the charity single "We Are the World," which sold millions of copies in 1985.**

# MEDIA MUSIC

Among the highest-earning musical careers are those in the media, such as writing TV theme tunes or advertising jingles. A jingle writer is usually a musician with a background in songwriting or composition. The main responsibility is for the music to represent the advertiser, as the advertiser directs, so the ability to understand and stick to the advertiser's brief (precise instructions) is essential. The most successful jingle writers are skilled in all styles of music: an advertiser's requirements may call for a knowledge of classical orchestral music, jazz, classic pop and rock styles, right up to the hippest of new alternative and dance music. Not many people with such a wide knowledge of music exist, let alone musicians who can play and arrange such music.

Writers of media music are more likely to work on their own or as a part of their own small company: few companies employ such staff on a full-time basis. Many jingle writers have their own studio facilities and knowledge and experience working to a specific **budget**—the amount of money available for a particular project. For example, a good jingle musician will know how to produce a convincing orchestral sound using digital sampling techniques (see box on page 32) on those occasions when not enough money is available to record a real orchestra.

wish to do this must be members of one of the musicians' unions in Hollywood, which have a strong hold on the availability of work in this field. Competition for this work is fierce even for established session musicians, and the availability of steady work largely depends on the current state of the film industry. There are certain bonuses though: a prominent or solo spot in a film recording can earn a musician a small "residual"—a percentage of a film's profits. Such opportunities most likely go to musicians who have spent 15 or 20 years working the session circuits.

Although not quite so well paid as film sessions, theater pit orchestras can provide a regular income for session musicians. New York's Broadway shows tend to attract the best session players, and accordingly they are paid the most money. Yet the major downside is that the work can become rather repetitive, playing the same music night after night, especially on long-running shows.

### Teaching music

The unsung heroes of the music world are the professional teachers.

The best music educators are those who have dedicated themselves to just that—music education. Yet despite the efforts of Lowell Mason (see pages 10–11), music is the first subject to be cut in U.S. public schools, and the salary for public

**Above: The orchestra pit before a show at the London Coliseum theater. Despite the confines of space, the orchestra sets up in a similar way to a concert orchestra, with the conductor in the middle, facing the stage.**

**Left: A teacher guides a class of students through a violin composition.**

# MUSIC THERAPY

A relatively recent occupation, and one that is continuing to grow in popularity, is music therapy. It is a health profession in which music is used as a treatment for various types of disabilities. Music therapists work in a number of different settings: general and psychiatric hospitals; community mental health agencies; substance- (drug-) abuse programs; tumor treatment centers; pain- and stress-management clinics; correctional institutions or prisons; day-care centers; nursing homes; schools; and private practices. The job usually involves providing support and therapy services to people with psychiatric disorders, physical and developmental disabilities, speech and hearing impairments, or nerve damage.

People involved in music therapy should have a genuine interest in others and a desire to help them in order to establish caring and professional relationships with their patients. Music therapists need to be musicians as well as therapists, so a background in and love of music are also essential.

To work as a music therapist requires a formal education. An increasing number of colleges offer undergraduate degrees in music therapy. A student will have to take not only music courses but others in psychology, biology, and social and behavioral sciences. Those considering a career in music therapy are also advised to gain experience through volunteer

**Above: A music therapist helps a child play a drum in a class for the disabled in Arnstadt, Germany.**

work in nursing homes, camps for children with disabilities, and other environments that cater to people with disabilities.

---

school teachers is usually not as good as in higher education or private teaching (see page 26). So teaching in schools is often seen as a last resort.

A career in music education requires not only a love of music but also a strong urge to communicate and teach people about music. A good teacher must truly desire his or her students to improve and succeed.

At the elementary or high-school levels the job can be frustrating since some children and teenagers may not view music classes as being important to their futures. On the other hand, there are great rewards in teaching music at this level. Inspiring and encouraging young students to discover their musical talents and develop their skills can give them an early belief in their abilities and an enduring appreciation of music that can make a huge difference to their future success in music or their enjoyment of life in general.

## Higher-level music education

Teaching music at universities or colleges is different because the students are already committed to learning about music. However, higher qualifications are necessary—in most cases a PhD or DMA (Doctor of Musical Arts)—to get a teaching job at this level. Music teachers are expected not only to teach but also to have their work published. The pay tends to be better than at the high-school level, and usually fewer teaching hours are demanded, allowing teachers to pursue their musical interests outside teaching.

Left: A voice teacher demonstrates how to breathe deeply from the stomach in order to sustain one's breath while singing.

Musicians dedicated to performing can sometimes get a college teaching position to add to their performance income. Other higher-education teaching fields include music history, music theory and composition, and music technology (see page 13).

Careers in administration can also be found in music education. Behind any well run music institution or department is an administrative staff that knows about music, the music world, and the people in it. Typical duties can involve public relations, community outreach, fund-raising, concert programing, and general management. The most successful candidates tend to be those with degrees in both music and business.

### Private teaching

Of course, teaching students to sing or play an instrument is also done outside the school system through private music lessons. Anyone wishing to teach outside of an educational institution should advertise their services in a local newspaper or magazine or on bulletin boards in local music shops, supermarkets, or anywhere that might be seen by those interested in their services.

Piano and guitar are the most common instruments to be taught privately because they are the most popular among people who want to learn an instrument. However, any instrument can be taught privately, depending on local demand. For example, in a small community one might do well as a piano teacher, but

---

## Piano and guitar are the most common instruments to be taught privately

---

setting oneself up as an oboe teacher could be risky, since those wanting to learn the oboe will probably be few and far between. Yet in a large city, being a piano teacher might be more risky, since there will be competition from many other piano teachers, and an oboe teacher might therefore face less competition and fare better.

The ability to teach more than one instrument is also an advantage. Yet success will often depend on having impressive musical credentials and establishing a good reputation, which may take time. But once a teacher has acquired enough satisfied students, recommendations by word of mouth may make advertising unnecessary.

## Other music careers

Careers as a composer or songwriter are difficult to predict and rely on great self-motivation. Classical composers should send their work to music conservatories and conductors, whereas commercial songwriters must send their material by way of a demo to bands, record companies, and music publishers. Music business careers—including artist management (see pages 33–34), marketing (see pages 37–39), **plugging** (see pages 39–40), promoters and agents (see page 42), tour managers and road crew (see page 43), and A&R (see pages 45–46)—are discussed in Chapters 3 and 4. Recording studio careers, including tape operators (see pages 53–54), engineers (see pages 54–55), and producers (see pages 55–57), are covered in Chapter 5.

# THE PROFESSIONAL DJ

Traditionally, a disk jockey was someone who broadcast music over the radio. The job involved both selecting the music to be played and acting as a voice-over "link" between songs. Since U.S. radio is mostly commercial, funding for radio stations came mainly from advertisers, so DJ's links were usually advertisements. This resulted in the birth of the "personality" DJ, whose job was to entertain the audience as well as to provide it with music.

Since the DJ is essentially a performer, there are no definite career routes. Many start off working unpaid on school, college, or hospital radio stations from where they can gain professional opportunities in low-key spots on commercial radio stations. Another start-off point for a DJ is to take a low-paid job as assistant to the producer and work up through the ranks. From there success depends on the DJ's ability to find an audience. Competition for radio jobs is intense, so DJs who are well-connected and experienced will always have an advantage.

In the 1950s a different type of DJ emerged. Instead of airing records on the radio, the DJ selected and played them to live audiences dancing in nightclubs. This phenomenon spread gradually with the "Go-Gos" of the 1960s, "disco" in the 1970s, and the hugely popular club culture of the 1990s. The hippest club DJs have always had an influence over the cutting edge of dance music. Now, a top club DJ can become a household name and earn as much as a pop star. Some take on joint careers as producers, "remixing" the music of other artists, or becoming chart stars in their own right.

**Above: DJ and recording artist Fatboy Slim performing at the Brixton Academy club in London, England.**

Making it as a top club DJ is about as unpredictable and difficult as becoming a pop star. Yet even small towns are likely to have clubs, so there is clearly a role and a living to be made for DJs with modest expectations. The most successful DJs will get into the collective minds of a club audience and keep a finger on the pulse of changing trends in music.

# CHAPTER 3

# The Music Business

Since the arrival of rock 'n' roll in the 1950s the music business has grown from a money maker to a multibillion dollar monster in which artists and others are capable of making vast fortunes.

Throughout the ages, from the groups of minstrels who earned their keep traveling from town to town playing music and singing, to the early classical composers who sought the patronage of the aristocracy, there have always been those who have viewed music as a business rather than as art or entertainment. However, it was not until the turn of the 20th century that music began to produce a definable "industry" in which both the artists and those behind the scenes were capable of earning vast fortunes. A century later music and its associated merchandise form one branch of a massive entertainment economy that is worth billions of dollars every year.

**Above: The end of the line for the music companies is the fans who spend millions of dollars each year on CDs, concert tickets, and a whole range of music memorabilia.**

## Tin Pan Alley and beyond

The U.S. music business first centered itself on the East Coast in New York City and was based around a musical locale that became known as Tin Pan Alley. This was the nickname of New York's 28th Street, between Fifth Avenue and Broadway in Manhattan, where the earliest music publishers were based. The name came from the "tin pan" sound of the pianos as they were pounded by songwriters and song **pluggers** demonstrating their new tunes to would-be publishers (see Volume 7, pages 19–20).

The term "Tin Pan Alley" also came to mean the commercial music made by the songwriters of popular sentimental ballads, dance music, and comedy vaudeville numbers. By the 1930s, when Tin Pan Alley was at its peak, the name had become synonymous with all forms of white American popular music of the time.

The most profitable commercial product of early Tin Pan Alley was sheet music for people to play at home. Families made their own entertainment, sometimes singing songs around the piano in the evenings. This is where the term "music publisher" originally came from—the days when music really was only published on paper. The birth of a successful new industry attracted songwriters, composers, and lyricists, all of whom labored to produce popular new tunes to meet an increasing home-based demand.

## Records and radio

By the start of World War II popular music was already beginning to change, with **records**, radio, and, later, TV taking over from sheet music sales. With recorded music available on these various mediums families and private individuals at home became less interested in making music for themselves. The greater availability of music through these mediums after World War II effectively killed off the notion of Tin Pan Alley as a single musical source. Nevertheless, the Broadway area remained an important center for America's music business.

In the 1950s remnants of Tin Pan Alley working practices were continuing to prove successful at a number of "songwriting factories,"

**Below: The Brill Building on Broadway, New York City, where many of the greatest hits of the rock 'n' roll era were composed.**

**Above: Jerry Leiber and Mike Stoller were one of the most successful pop songwriting partnerships of the 1960s.**

the best known of which was the Brill Building, located at 1619 Broadway. It was here that classic songwriters of the time—such as Jerry Leiber (b. 1933) and Mike Stoller (b. 1933), who wrote "Hound Dog" and "Jailhouse Rock" for Elvis Presley; Gerry Goffin (b. 1939) and Carole King (b. 1942), who wrote "The Loco-Motion" and "A Natural Woman"; Barry Mann (b. 1939) and Cynthia Weill (b. 1939), who wrote "You've Lost That Lovin' Feeling" and "Saturday Night at the Movies"; and Neil Sedaka (b. 1939), who wrote "Breaking Up Is Hard to Do"—continued the production-line approach to songwriting, creating many of the greatest hits of the pop era (see Volume 6, pages 16–17).

### Music publishing

After the heyday of Tin Pan Alley music publishers found that they had to adapt to a world of changing technology. By the 1920s sheet-music sales began to dwindle as sales of records began to take off in a big way. But since recordings still relied on the use of an original published work, it stood to reason that the publishers

of these songs were entitled to payment of some kind. Since then, payments for songs used either on recordings or for public performance have been the main source of income for music publishers.

Just as record labels are always on the lookout for the "next big thing," so are music publishers eager to sign up future songwriting talent. A typical deal for an unknown songwriter would involve payment of an **advance** against a share of future **royalties**. While on the surface it may not seem as if the publishers are doing too much to earn their cut (percentage), there are several advantages for a musician in working with them. First, with the business organization in place it is easier for a large publisher to collect songwriting royalties. Additionally, a part of the publisher's job is to try to "place" the songs with suitable recording artists, thereby earning further income.

When a songwriter signs a deal with a music publisher, a part of the contract defines the "territories" in which the publisher has responsibility. If the company owns world rights, a normal practice is to license or subpublish the songs in different countries or continents. Publishing laws differ according to the territory; and since few U.S. publishers are experts in international law, it usually makes good sense to have the songs published by a company with suitable local experience and expertise. At the top end of the business the modern-day music publisher often operates as a part of a record company.

### Protecting the artist

The story of a young, up-and-coming musician signing a contract that subsequently proves to have been ill-advised is nothing new in the world of music. After all, at the start of their careers most musicians know little about royalties, percentages, and advances. That is why nowadays it is rare for a person to sign an important contract without the assistance of a music business lawyer.

While there is not too much the law can do to protect a musician from making a poor business decision, there are formal ways in which an artist's music can be protected. This process is known as **copyright**, and it can work in a number of different ways.

The most common copyright dispute comes from one artist claiming that another has copied one of his or her original songs. This

**Below: The Chiffons, whose 1963 song "He's So Fine" was allegedly "rewritten" by George Harrison as "My Sweet Lord."**

is against the law pretty much everywhere in the world. But there can be a fine line between being inspired by a song and "borrowing" too heavily from it.

In one famous example George Harrison of the Beatles was found guilty of "**plagiarism**" when the tune for his worldwide 1971 hit "My Sweet Lord" was alleged to have been a "rewrite" of a song called "He's So Fine"—a hit in 1963 for the Chiffons. Although the judge accepted that he may have "subconsciously adapted" the song, Harrison was found guilty and forced to pay a half million dollars to Bright Tunes, the publisher of "He's So Fine."

## ASCAP and BMI

When an artist writes a piece of music, he or she is entitled to both mechanical and performance copyright protection. Mechanical copyright refers to an original song that features on a commercial release, such as a **CD** or **cassette**. Each time an album is "pressed"—that is, when a copy of a CD, cassette, or vinyl record is manufactured—the songwriter (or publisher) is eligible for a small percentage of the sales price. These fees are registered on forms completed at the album-pressing plant. A musician wishing to record someone else's song needs to file a request for a mechanical license from the publisher of the song so that the writer will receive payment.

The other kind of copyright covers the public performance of a song. The writer of any piece of music that is played on the radio, TV, cinema, or in any other public place is entitled to a performance payment. In the case of some popular composers this alone can bring in millions of dollars each year. This is one reason why the songwriters in a band can earn so

# DIGITAL SAMPLING

One of the key areas of concern over copyright, as well as one of the most important technical developments of the past two decades, has been the birth and evolution of digital sampling. At its simplest, a digital sampler is a keyboard that is equipped to record and play back digital sounds.

Although in principle sampling has dominated recorded pop music since its beginnings, its relevant history can be traced back to the 1960s and an instrument called the Mellotron. It worked in fundamentally the same way as a sampler except that each key was linked to a cartridge holding a loop of magnetic tape that contained a pre-recorded sample of a real instrument playing that same note.

The first commercially available digital sampling system was the Fairlight CMI, which was developed in 1979. Although it was used widely, at a cost of $160,000 for a full system only the wealthiest producers and musicians could afford it. Rapid developments in

technology have brought prices down to the point where it is now possible to buy a sampling keyboard with extensive editing facilities and 50 times as much "on-board" memory as the Fairlight all for less than $1,000.

As well as providing a means for imitating real instruments, sampling developed in a rather unexpected way, as dance music producers began to

**Above: Robbie Williams' 1998 hit "Millennium" famously featured a James Bond movie theme tune.**

digitally record and play back snatches or **loops** of existing songs and build them into their own music. On the negative side this has led to a number of legal cases where artists have recognized their own music used in other more recent recordings, often without permission. On the positive side it has meant that old classic tunes of the 1960s, 1970s, and 1980s have been updated and subsequently heard by an entirely new audience.

The most common use for this approach is in programming drum loops. One particular **drum fill**—on the James Brown track "Funky Drummer" played by Clyde Stubblefield—has been featured on numerous dance and rap hits over the past 15 years.

One of the most famous examples of sampling in recent years was the use of the theme to the James Bond movie *You Only Live Twice* in former Take That singer Robbie Williams' 1998 hit single "Millennium."

**Above: Clyde Stubblefield—the most sampled drummer in rock 'n' roll.**

much more money than those who just play. Performance payments are collected based on forms completed by the TV or radio stations. All U.S. commercial songwriters or publishers belong to one of two organizations: ASCAP (the American Society of Composers, Authors, and Publishers) or BMI (Broadcast Music, Incorporated). Both are nonprofit bodies and exist only to protect the interests of their members.

## Artists and managers

For the past half century most music stars have owed at least a part of their success to people working on their behalf behind the scenes. The most important of these figures is the manager. Although often popularly portrayed as seedy, untrustworthy, and ever looking for new ways to rip-off clients (and there are many examples to back up that view), the

**Above: Beatles manager Brian Epstein (center) relaxes with John Lennon (left) and Ringo Starr (right) in Paris in 1964.**

simple fact is that in an age when a popular band can employ a staff of hundreds and turn over millions of dollars a year, they are a necessity.

The precise relationship between artist and manager will be different in every case, but the essential task of the manager is to take care of administering the business, freeing up the artist to concentrate on the music itself. This clearly means that artists rely heavily on the manager for even the most basic of tasks: organizing their daily affairs, making business decisions on their behalfs, and ensuring that they are where they are supposed to be at any given time.

The rewards for successful managers can be immense. Brian Epstein (1934–1967) was one of the most famous managers in pop history, having taken the Beatles from obscurity in Liverpool to the top of the charts worldwide. Although he

**Above: Colonel Tom Parker (right), also known as "the Colonel," poses for photographers with a young Elvis Presley.**

name. Like Epstein, Parker took a 25 percent cut of Elvis's earnings. He had absolute control over every aspect of Presley's career. It was Parker who continually encouraged Elvis's mediocre movie career and later supplied him with the middle-of-the-road songs that resulted in a decline in his career (Parker has been accused of hiring second-rate songwriters and taking a cut of their publishing royalties). Unbelievably, in 1967 Parker renegotiated his contract with Elvis, upping his cut to 50 percent!

Nevertheless, Parker was also very useful for Elvis. He looked after Elvis's career while he was away in Germany with the U.S. Army for 18 months, never allowing his name to be out of the papers and magazines. He never missed an opportunity to publicize his one and only client. He made sure that the fees Elvis received for his movies remained as high as

## Some 25 years after his death Elvis Presley was still worth millions of dollars

they possibly could be. Though this was all good for his client, there is no doubt that it was all good for Parker too. His love of money was legendary. As one of Elvis's former aides once quipped, "From the time he signed with Parker to the time he died, Elvis never did anything for free."

After Presley's death a reporter asked the Colonel what he was going to do. "I'm gonna carry on managing Elvis," came the reply. Even now, some quarter of a century after his death, the Elvis industry continues to turn over millions of dollars a year.

Over the past two decades rock and pop music have become

had little to do with musical decisions, Epstein's influence in other matters was big, and his payment was as much as 25 percent of the band's earnings.

A more notorious example is that of Colonel Tom Parker (1909–1997), the man who managed and guided Elvis Presley throughout his life as the world's most famous singer. Parker took over Elvis's affairs in 1956, the year Presley became a household

# THE SAGA OF THE SEX PISTOLS

Left: Malcolm McLaren (third from right) watches as the Sex Pistols sign their recording contract with the A&M record label outside London's Buckingham Palace in March 1977.

Some band managers, especially those who claim an original artistic vision, exert a viselike grip over their artists, viewing them as little more than employees. One of the most famous examples of this occurred in the mid-1970s, when the group the Sex Pistols was unleashed on the world by their manager Malcolm McLaren (b. 1946). Before the Pistols were formed, McLaren had run a clothing shop called "Sex" in London's Kings Road with his wife, the fashion designer Vivienne Westwood. The store became well known for its incredibly hip "bondage" stock—torn T-shirts with controversial logos; trousers with straps, buckles, and zips; and other items complete with safety pins—and attracted a hard core of young "alternative" types who frequently visited the store. McLaren planned to create something of a musical equivalent to the clothes sold in the shop. He decided to design and market a band on its aggressive appearance, sound, and attitude, courting controversy wherever possible.

Emerging from the motley assortment who hung around the shop, the Sex Pistols quickly made a name in London's music press as leaders of the **punk** rock movement. Things took off when McLaren booked them a guest spot on an early evening London TV news program. By swearing at their host and behaving in an obnoxious manner, they created such a public outrage that on the following morning they found themselves on the front pages of the national newspapers. They were yet to even set foot in a recording studio.

Such publicity made them a hot property in the music business, creating a bidding war among the major record labels. McLaren signed them to the famous EMI label, which gave them a large advance on future royalties—a payment up front for music that would be sold later. At the same time, McLaren continued to stir up the tabloid press with controversial stories, so much so that EMI's conservative shareholders demanded the band be thrown off the label.

McLaren and the Sex Pistols came out of the EMI deal having recorded one single—the classic "Anarchy in the UK"—and kept their five-figure advance. They repeated the process with A&M Records, again coming out of it with a substantial amount of money without having done any recording work at all.

They finally signed a deal with Richard Branson's Virgin label. Their crowning achievement came in June 1977, when they coincided their second single, "God Save the Queen," with Queen Elizabeth II's Silver Jubilee celebrations. Once again, the establishment rose to McLaren's bait, with tabloid newspapers reaching hysteria in their criticism of the timing of the single, the nature of the lyrics (though it was definitely not a version of the British national anthem), and the cover, which portrayed the Queen wearing the punk's hallmark safety pin through her nose. It was the kind of publicity that no amount of marketing could ever hope to match. The single, of course, went straight into the charts.

"respectable," and it is now not uncommon for managers to have formal qualifications, such as a degree in business administration, or come from associated professions like law and accounting.

## Albums and singles

Whatever the type of music in question, successful artists take the greater part of their income from sales of their recordings, which fall into two distinct categories: the single and the album. When record sales first became widespread during the 1920s, an artist would periodically "cut a side." Since records could be played on both sides, this meant that each record contained two songs. Unlike in later years, though, neither was necessarily considered to be the "main" song.

**Above: An original vinyl record album containing 12 10-inch 78 rpm records.**

It was very difficult, however, to present classical music on this new medium, since some symphonies or operas could last for several hours.

# THE PAYOLA SCANDAL

During the second half of the 1950s, as radio made music for young people more popular and record sales boomed, DJs became more crucial to the record companies. A record played on the radio one evening could mean lines to buy it at the record stores the following morning. In 1955 *Billboard* magazine started a chart of the top 100 best-selling records to keep track of the rising sales of 7-inch singles. One of the most popular DJs, Alan Freed (1926–1965), who had radio shows in Cleveland and New York, was so influential among teenagers that he also did personal appearances at record stores and organized live shows with bands like Fats Domino, Jackie Wilson, the Drifters, and Chuck Berry.

But the music scene at this time was full of jealousy and intolerance, and the long-established companies were suddenly being overrun by newcomers, eager to cash in on the rising popularity among teenagers of music like rhythm and blues and rock 'n' roll. Freed's popularity and influence made him a target for those conservative elements in the music business. He was accused of corrupting American youth by playing this new wild music, causing riots at dances in the process, and accepting bribes—also known as payola—in return for playing particular records on his show to improve their sales. Although this was common practice among most DJs at the time, Freed was convicted on two counts of bribery and was fined and given a suspended jail sentence.

Despite his position as one of the premier rock 'n' roll DJs, Freed remains forever associated with this scandal.

**Above: Alan Freed arrives at court in Boston to face charges of causing a riot in 1958.**

onto the charts became increasingly important in its own right. Music shows on radio and TV turned the top 20 singles into a major weekly event for teenagers. For an artist, getting on the chart meant more exposure, more sales, and an even higher chart position. This realization has pretty well governed the sale of pop music singles ever since.

Long-playing albums (LPs) first became popular in the 1950s. For pop music, at least, at this time they comprised little more than a few hit singles bundled together with a load of other less memorable songs. It wasn't until the decade that followed that the notion of the album as a body of work in its own right became widely recognized through such milestones as the Beatles' *Revolver* and *Sgt. Pepper's Lonely Hearts Club Band* albums. The latter was even more extraordinary in that it had no relationship to the band's phenomenal success on the singles charts around the world: no track from the album was intended for release as a single.

Since this time the album format, which now also includes CD albums, has been the creative benchmark by which most artists have been judged.

The approach taken was to break the complete original piece up into smaller pieces that could then be fitted on one side of a record. The sleeves for each of these records were then bound together like pages in an album. Thus the original albums were quite literally "albums," often containing 20 or more records. It wasn't until the 1950s, when manufacturing technology had improved, that "long-playing" records, featuring six or more songs on each side, began to appear. By the middle of the 1960s albums had become important articles in their own right: before this time the industry had concentrated mainly on the "single."

From the 1940s onward the selling of recorded music revolved around the idea of "hit parade" charts. Some of them were based on sales, others on radio and jukebox airplay. Yet what had first begun as a simple measure of popularity gradually developed into an end in itself—the simple act of getting

**Above: The Beatles' *Sgt. Pepper's Lonely Hearts Club Band* LP was one of the first albums with no tracks intended for release as a single.**

### Selling the product

The promotion and marketing departments of a record company are crucial to the running of the music economy. They let the world know about their products, whether in the pop, jazz, or classical worlds.

A new release by a major artist will always be accompanied by a serious marketing campaign, in many cases costing the record company many times as much as the recording and production of the music. The word "campaign" is apt here, since to be successful it has to be planned and executed with military precision.

The most important tool at the marketing person's disposal is the media. At one time the radio disk jockey had the power to make or break a new record; now he is just one of a number of targets. TV is likely to play a much more important role: videos, advertising, and appearances on high-profile shows are all part of the promotion game, and all have to be planned months in advance. The traditional paper poster is also still an important marketing tool. Nowadays, though, no new pop release can even be contemplated without a dedicated Web page: there is no question that

# THE BIRTH OF THE POP VIDEO

Marketing refers to the way in which a piece of music or an album is promoted. At one time, a typical campaign would entail putting up posters, advertising in the music press, and enticing disk jockeys and radio producers to play the music. All this changed in the summer of 1981, when MTV—Music Television—hit the cable and satellite airwaves for the first time.

From the mid-1970s the wealthier successful groups began to make short films to accompany their releases. This was largely so they could be shown on pop chart shows across the world without having to perform (or mime) on the show in person. One of the first noteworthy "videos" to be used in this way was made to promote Queen's 1975 hit "Bohemian Rhapsody."

The idea behind MTV was simplicity itself: wall-to-wall promotional videos presented by a variety of young, fashionable, good-looking "VJs"—video jockeys. At first the idea met with opposition from some record companies that refused to offer their videos without receiving some sort of payment: they felt aggrieved that they were, in effect, financing the output of a TV station (in effect, MTV was the first station designed with an agenda of ONLY playing commercials). As MTV inevitably took off, hostility quickly wilted as record companies saw the effect on sales of the records as well as on the videos that were being played on the station. From that point onward it was clear that a song had even more chance of being a hit with an accompanying video.

The way in which artists or musicians approach making a music video often reflects their own music. Those who consider themselves serious, credible artists generally want a video that creates the same message; for simple commercial music images of the singer or band filmed performing the song are usually enough.

Since making a music video is a little like making a short feature film, the most important figure in the process is the director. He or she is usually responsible for coming up with the idea for the content and getting that vision down on film. Although this may be seen as a slightly frivolous job for an ambitious film maker, most video directors take these roles very seriously; some of Hollywood's finest young directors have used music videos as a calling card to get a foothold in the world of "real" movies.

Even at the lowest level, making a music video is never cheap. Hiring a director, film crew, editing suites, props, and locations can cost as much if not more than recording the music itself.

**Above: A director and his assistant editing a pop video in the studio.**

Left: Posters for concerts and albums on city streets— especially near shops and concert halls— are very useful for targeting a particular local audience.

the Internet will play an increasingly important role in both the marketing and selling of music.

When a major artist has a new album ready for release, the wheels of the marketing department will start turning months before the all-important release date. Promotional copies of the album will have been sent out to all the important disk jockeys or music critics several months beforehand. The timing is critical here: in an ideal world monthly music magazines will have been able to feature articles and reviews several weeks in advance of the actual release, building up anticipation and turning it into an "event."

## Targeting the right audience

One of the main functions of any marketing department—whatever the product being sold—is in targeting and finding the right audience. This has become an increasingly difficult and skilled art to master. At one time, pop music was the sole domain of teenagers, making it easier for music promoters to find their target audiences. Yet as pop and rock have aged, so has their audience: many attributed the success of Oasis to their ability to appeal both to young rock fans and "50-somethings" who were old enough to remember the Beatles from the first time around. Markets have also become more fragmented, with magazines, films, and TV shows designed to appeal to definable groups of society. Marketing experts must be able to decide which of these areas are most appropriate and therefore effective to target.

Another important part of every music release is employing the services of a "plugger." The sole task of a plugger is to get the product directly into the hands of the right people. For example, in the case of some of the biggest dance hits influential club DJs need to be targeted well in advance. Many hip, cutting-edge dancefloor hits are popular in clubland for months before the music is even available to the buying public: this explains the phenomenon of the unknown artist shooting straight to the top of the charts, seemingly without any publicity.

The plugger must also target radio DJs as well as the radio station's producers: nowadays, the radio DJ is often nothing more than a presenter who plays the records he or she is told to by the producer. Most radio stations have "playlists," which highlight current releases that the station intends to play. Clearly, getting on a playlist can make the difference between success or failure. Plugging is one of the most aggressive forms of salesmanship in the music world; it can literally mean waiting around outside a studio and being a real nuisance until the product is delivered to the right person.

## Distribution and retailing

Of course, crucial to the whole success of a new release is the matter of distribution—getting the music onto the streets. If consumers cannot walk into a music store and find the product on the shelves, then the whole effort is wasted. While most of the major labels have their own distribution networks in place, smaller labels rely on specialized distribution companies, which take on the responsibility of getting the products into the music stores.

Distribution managers work closely with the major music chains. While at one time distributors had to deal with large numbers of independent stores,

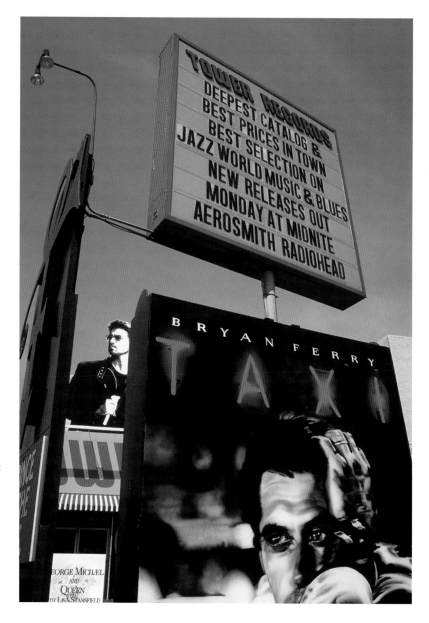

the vast majority of consumers now buy their music from a relatively small core of outlets. For example, the Tower Records chain is responsible for a significant proportion of all music sold in the United States. Consequently, these stores have a considerable influence on record companies. The task of distribution is made easier because sales to these large corporations are centralized— they decide themselves the quantities that are sent to their various stores. They are also able to take advantage of economies of scale—because they buy such a large volume of music,

**Above: The Tower Records chain has thousands of branches, such as this one in Los Angeles, and sells so many CDs that it has a major influence on record companies.**

Left: In the 1990s the U.S. band the Grateful Dead made more money from merchandising than any other rock 'n' roll band on the circuit.

Below: Sales of merchandise—T-shirts, badges, posters—often make up for money lost through the high costs of touring.

they will expect to pay the record company a lower price per unit and therefore offer better retail prices to their customers.

Another recent avenue of distribution and retailing is through the Internet. Nowadays there are many websites that offer on-line shopping for CDs and other formats of music. The customer merely has to place an order through the Internet to receive the desired product.

## Going on the road

When an artist or musician goes on tour, there are a number of crucial people, apart from the musicians, who make the whole process possible. Each takes his or her own cut of the profits, meaning that unless the artist is a major concert draw, touring is not always the most profitable part of the business. Often, tours are simply written off as a necessary part of promoting a new recording. The

record company might lose money on a tour, but in the long run this loss will be more than made up for in music sales. Merchandising—the selling of T-shirts, posters, badges, and other paraphernalia—is also a highly lucrative way of bolstering income, especially since such items can typically have up to 500-percent markup.

## Agents and promoters

Many people muddle the roles of the agent and promoter. Although they are quite distinct, specific duties do often overlap. The job of the agent is to book and organize performance dates. He or she must find venues that are appropriate to the type of music being played and of a size that matches the likely demand for tickets. The promoter, on the other hand, is concerned with the details of a specific concert; for example, the hiring of facilities and necessary equipment,

the provision of security, insurance, advertising, and marketing. Both parties are likely to take between 10 and 25 percent of the artist's fee.

The artist's fee can be calculated in several different ways. Traditionally, the agent would agree on a flat fee with the venue owner/manager or promoter. This would reflect the artist's market value and could alter according to their popularity.

At the highest level it is more common nowadays for the artist to take a percentage of the price of every ticket that is sold. This is usually referred to as a "percentage of the **gross**." Where the success of the event is in any doubt, some agents agree on a "guaranteed minimum" payment. This means that in exchange for a lower artist percentage the promoter agrees to a minimum figure that will be paid even if ticket sales fail to cover the fee.

**Below: Roadies— who are mainly responsible for unloading equipment and setting it up on stage—are an essential part of going on the road.**

**Above: Double basses being unloaded from their cases backstage at Avery Fisher Hall in New York City. A few hours later they would be used in a performance by the London Symphony Orchestra.**

In either case it is essential that both agent and promoter have a good feel for what the public wants to see and how much it is prepared to pay for the privilege.

### Tour staff

The members of the artist's tour crew can be described as the footsoldiers of live music. The head of the team is the tour manager. This is an important role; and as the name suggests, he or she is responsible for the everyday running of the entire operation. This means making travel arrangements, managing the road crew, keeping the artist happy, and making sure that **gig** promoters have made provisions for security and equipment. Good tour managers have to be able to juggle numerous tasks, maintain a firm grip on those under their control, and also deal

with problems as they arise using tact and diplomacy, often while under extreme pressure. Getting on with everyone is often the most important quality in a good road manager.

The road crew (or "roadies," as they are known) are responsible for loading and unloading equipment and setting it up on stage—and, of course, for taking it down after the show. Some roadies are also music technicians responsible for preparing an instrument for use on stage: this can include anything from tuning the instrument and ensuring that connections work to getting specific sounds from special effects units. These jobs may not seem terribly glamorous, and long tours can be grueling and incredibly hard work, but a good road crew is essential to ensure that a tour is carried off as smoothly as possible.

# CHAPTER 4

# The Growth of the Record Company

In the music industry record companies are responsible for everything from developing new talent to promoting CDs. Over the past century they have also played a major role in making music one of the world's most important entertainment products.

Record companies are at the very heart of the music industry. They are responsible for organizing all the steps in the production and promotion process of selling music. These steps include signing new talent; recording the music; putting the music on **CD**, **cassette** tape, and vinyl **record**; promoting the artist and the music; and finally distributing the music to retail outlets or stores across the world. Within a record company all the steps are carried out by different departments, but it is not unusual for some steps to be assigned to outside organizations.

**Above: Music stores are the main places where record companies sell their products.**

44

Left: Alan McGee, one of the most successful A&R executives in the music industry. As the head of Creation Records, he represented the band Oasis. Early in 2000 he launched a new record company called Poptones.

The record company staff who scout (search) for and sign new talent work in the artist-and-**repertoire** department (usually known as "A&R"). Recording and producing music takes place in the company's recording studio—although outside studios often provide both services for record companies.

Teams dedicated to deciding how a product should be presented and sold to the public work in the marketing and promotion departments. Printing and pressing plants manufacture the albums, covers, and any booklets. Finally, a distribution network makes sure that the product, such as a CD, is made available in music stores.

### The A&R executive

For musicians wanting to sign with a record company, the A&R executive is initially the most important person in the recording process. A typical day in the life of an A&R executive begins by sifting through stacks of mail, which usually includes a vast quantity of demonstration (**demo**) tapes and CDs from unsigned bands. Although only a very few artists are discovered in this way, the A&R executive has to give each demo a quick listen—even if it is for only ten seconds—just in case he or she hears something worthwhile.

From a musician's point of view an approach that is more likely to meet with success requires getting some form of representation. An artist's manager who is known in the music business will be able to make an appointment with an A&R executive.

## Catching the ear of an A&R executive is every young musician's dream

Since the A&R executive has to be in step or just ahead of new trends, he or she has to stay in close contact with promoters of small cult venues. The reason for this is that if an unsigned band is continually drawing large crowds, then the A&R executive has to find out first hand why the band is

Left: A gramophone, seen here, was the first popular instrument to play prerecorded music. The gramophone was operated by winding an arm on the side. This would rotate the turntable on which the record sat. The sound on the rotating record was then picked up by the stylus (needle), which fed the sound to the large horn that amplified (made louder) the sound.

so appealing. For the same reason, the A&R executive has to keep an eye on what is going on in other record companies, both big and small.

Because almost all A&R executives are based in a major city, like New York or Los Angeles, most evenings are taken up seeing live acts. In a busy evening it might be possible for an A&R executive to take in five or six **gigs**, staying at each one for only a couple of numbers. Most of the time A&R executives are only interested in acts that they have heard about on the music-business grapevine.

There is no doubt that A&R is a tough job: like stockbrokers, the A&R executive succeeds or fails by the **professional** choices he or she makes. The best A&R executives might be given their own labels to run within a company and make it right to the very top of the industry.

## Labels as companies

Ever since the beginning of the 20th century the music industry has been run by record companies, or "labels."

The terms "company" and "label" are often used interchangeably and in many cases amount to the same thing.

The term "label" is a leftover from the earliest days of the recording industry. It originally referred to the circular piece of paper that was pasted onto the center of each vinyl record.

DREAMS OF LONG AGO
COMPOSED BY ENRICO CARUSO
Sung by CARUSO on VICTOR RECORD No 88376

OTHER SONGS BY CARUSO
With English and Italian Words
THE SONG OF SPITE (Canzona a Dispietto)
OLDEN TIMES (Tiempo Antico)
THE FORSAKEN WINDOW (Fenesta Abbandunata)

ENGLISH VERSION by EARL CARROLL

LEO FEIST NEW YORK

Left: This is an advertisement for Enrico Caruso's record *Dreams of Long Ago*, made by the Victor label. Caruso was the world's first recording star. As an opera singer he lent an air of respectability to the fledgling music industry.

On the label were printed details about the recording such as song title, artist, and songwriter or composer.

Nowadays, large record companies have several labels, or subsidiaries, to cater to various types of music, such as EMI's jazz label, Blue Note.

## Birth of the recording industry

The history of the recording industry begins in 1894 with the introduction in the U.S. of Emil Berliner's "record disk" and **gramophone** (see Volume 9, page 55). A German inventor who lived in America, Berliner understood the moneymaking potential of his new invention and accordingly set up representatives in the U.S. and Europe.

---

### Berliner, who invented the gramophone, started the first big record companies

---

Over the years these representatives founded what would become the first record companies in the world, including Victor in the U.S. and Deutsche Grammophon in Germany.

Until the early 1900s the gramophone, also called a phonograph, was seen mostly as a novelty item on which short recordings of small bands, comedy routines, or funny noises could be heard.

In 1902 the opera singer Enrico Caruso (1873–1921) started to make recordings for the gramophone. Despite the poor sound quality of these early recordings, the records became very popular and made Caruso history's first recording star. Other leading opera singers soon followed his example by recording famous **arias**.

Below: A record label for the single of the blues classic "I Ain't Superstitious" from the independent Chess company.

These opera singers helped give the early recording industry a much needed boost of respectability.

By the mid-1920s gramophones were commonplace, and thousands of records had been sold. Dance tunes out of Tin Pan Alley, such as Irving Berlin's "Alexander's Ragtime Band," became popular favorites (see Volume 7, pages 19-20). Also at this time the sound quality of recordings improved dramatically due to the introduction of the microphone.

## Rise of the independents

In the early years there were roughly two types of record companies, commonly known as "independent" and "major"—like Victor and Columbia. These terms continue today, although the distinctions are often vague. A major record company is basically a large corporation that produces and sells a lot of different types of music. An independent label is not only a smaller organization than a major label, but it also tends to focus on a certain style of music.

During the 1920s, when America was enjoying economic prosperity, there was a small but buoyant market for what was termed "race" music. Race music consisted of jazz and blues recordings aimed largely at—and performed mostly by—members of the black community.

Some of the early stars of this period, like guitarists Blind Blake and Blind Lemon Jefferson (see Volume 5, pages 28 and 30), were pioneers in their field and are now thought of as important figures in the history of American music. Yet they were all but ignored by an industry in which few African Americans were able to thrive.

When the Depression arrived in 1929, the majority of the major labels thought—either through ignorance or prejudice—that black people would no longer be able to afford records and so dropped their "race" labels. Because of this the independent companies jumped in to fill the gaps in the market left by the majors. These small companies were often set up by Jewish or European immigrants for whom blues and jazz were exciting new musical forms.

The typical independent label was run by just one or two individuals, usually with a great passion for the music they were releasing. They would take care of all the tasks from finding musicians right up to selling the records directly to the public.

**Below: Elvis Presley making one of his first recordings for the major label RCA.**

Although their aims were to make money, in many cases the overriding concern was one of creating and maintaining high artistic values.

## Influencing the majors

The independent labels later began to have an impact on the majors, which kept a close watch on the activities of the small labels throughout the 1940s and 1950s. The majors were quick to capitalize on any new trends or acts that the independent labels were successfully promoting.

A famous example of this involved Elvis Presley, who recorded a handful of local hits for the independent Sun label before being signed to the major RCA label, with which he achieved worldwide success.

> *Elvis started his career with an independent label but became famous with a major*

By the end of the 1940s it was the independents that led the way in most developments in American music, notably Chicago's Chess label in the world of blues and New York's Blue Note label for jazz. Gradually, these innovations filtered through to mainstream popular culture as they were taken up by the majors.

Rock 'n' roll in the 1950s, and later rock and soul in the 1960s and 1970s, had a huge impact on the music industry. These trends gave rise to many successful small labels, like Atlantic, Elektra, and Motown. By the late 1970s and 1980s, however, nearly all of them had been bought out by major record companies. For example, both Atlantic and Elektra are now part of Warner-EMI, and Motown is owned by Universal.

# BLUE NOTE RECORDS

The Blue Note label is perhaps the most famous independent record company of them all. Its story began in 1930, when a young German jazz fan named Alfred Lion (1909–1987) visited New York primarily to buy records unavailable in Europe: he returned with over 300 new releases. Nine years later, fleeing from Nazi Germany, Lion moved to the U.S., where he continued to pursue his interest in jazz. He made recordings in his spare time of pianists such as Meade "Lux" Lewis (1905–1964) and Albert Ammons (1907–1949). He made 50 copies of his recordings and sold each one personally—this was the birth of Blue Note Records. Shortly afterward, Francis Wolff, a colleague from Lion's homeland, joined him in the U.S., and from then on the label thrived.

By the end of the 1940s Blue Note had completely embraced the new bebop sound, introducing amazing new talents like Thelonious Monk and Bud Powell to the jazz world (see Volume 5, pages 56 to 57). However, it was the decade that followed that would mark out the label's lasting legacy.

In 1951, in search of a better sound for his releases, Lion was introduced to a young recording engineer named Rudy Van Gelder. This resulted in a completely new approach to recording small live jazz ensembles, as Van Gelder concentrated on pinpointing the most minute

**Above: German-born Alfred Lion, the founder of Blue Note. His jazz label became one of America's best known.**

details of the sound, such as the high-hat cymbals on the drum set. Such clarity was unknown at that time and set the standards for others to follow. Indeed, new music technology may have advanced beyond recognition since that time, but Van Gelder's Blue Note work still stands as a benchmark of quality recorded sound.

Blue Note's final innovation was in the way the music was presented. Since the bebop and "cool" jazz sounds mainly appealed to hip urban sophisticates, Lion reasoned that his record covers should reflect his market. So, he hired up-and-coming designers like the young Andy Warhol and Harold Feinstein to create a new look for his jackets. However, it was the arrival in 1956 of graphic designer Reid Miles that created the classic Blue Note look of cropped single-tone photographs with characteristic bold typography. You only needed to glance at a record cover to know that it was a Blue Note.

The label remained under the control of Lion and Wolff until the mid-1960s. Today, although a subsidiary of the Capitol label, the majority of Lion's classic recordings are still widely available. In 1991 a book of Reid Miles' finest album covers was published to great acclaim and popularity. Blue Note is now widely recognized as an important part of jazz history and consequently of American culture.

**Above: One of Reid Miles' unmistakable Blue Note album covers, reproduced for the CD cover.**

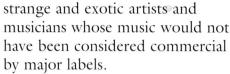

Above: Bruce Pavitt, a founder of the Seattle "grunge" label, Sub-Pop.

Below: Roger Ames (left) and Ken Berry celebrating the merger of Warner and EMI. Ames is chairman of Warner Music Group, and Berry is head of EMI.

## Second wave

A second wave of radical independent music companies started in the late 1970s, when many of the **punk** and **new wave** records of the period came out on one-man "bedroom" labels (the term "bedroom" refers to the common use of bedrooms as offices for these one-man labels). Many of these labels were little more than hobbies for their owners, who by and large released one or two records and then stopped. Nonetheless, this generated a creative energy that carried, providing outlets for many strange and exotic artists and musicians whose music would not have been considered commercial by major labels.

From time to time such small labels can be responsible for popularizing a certain type of new music, as was the case with Seattle's Sub-Pop label, which at the end of the 1980s defined the **"grunge"** sound that became successful the world over. In truth, however, while there will always be a niche for independent music, it becomes increasingly tough for small labels to compete on an equal footing with the commercial giants.

## Major advancements

Since the beginning of the 1980s the recording industry has continued to grow with the introduction of new developments in communication, such as the CD and later the Internet. During this same time the largest major record companies began taking a more aggressively global view of their markets, so that their biggest acts became popular across the globe.

## Independent labels remain an important source of new and innovative music

By the 1990s the major record companies accounted for around 75 percent of the world's music sales. Nowadays the major labels are in fact a part of just five enormous multi-national corporations. The largest of them is Warner-EMI, which is the result of a merger in January 2000 between the American Time-Warner group and Britain's EMI. Among their labels are the famed Warner, EMI, and Virgin brands.

The rest of the "big five" are Sony, Philips, Bertelsmann, and Universal. Most of them are heavily involved in both the entertainment and technology fields, and for all of them recorded music is just one of their many interests.

## Keeping it in the family

This multi-interest approach by the organizations that control the major labels allows for a kind of corporate "cross-fertilization" to take place. For example, it is increasingly common for an entertainment corporation's blockbuster movie to feature a hit song by one of its own stars.

A prime example of this is *Men in Black* (1996). The motion picture was produced by Columbia Pictures, and the movie's single, "Men in Black," was released by Columbia Records. Both organizations are owned by the Sony Corporation. And to complete the package, the film's star, rapper Will Smith, wrote and performed the single. In other words, the movie featured the song, the song was made into a video that featured the movie, and all three became huge hits, ultimately making a lot of money for Sony.

# MUSIC WEBSITES

The Internet has had more of an effect on the way in which we communicate and interact with one another than any other technical innovation since TV. Although it began in the 1960s as a way for U.S. military bases to communicate safely with each other, by the end of the 1990s the Internet had reached the world's mainstream.

Independent musicians and record companies were quick to see the potential for making their music and presence felt on the Web. **Home pages** containing information on bands and availability of music could be viewed by anyone on the Internet. As technology became faster, the same labels began to include snatches of sounds that could be **downloaded** from certain websites. Although this was slow at first, the emergence of the MP3 format (see page 67) drastically decreased the amount of time it took to download a near-CD-quality recording.

The major record companies also realized the potential of the Internet—however, some say they only took an interest when their **copyrights** were violated by Internet pirates, those who illegally **uploaded** commercial releases.

In the past, when "threatened" by new technology, the record industry has been able to throw its weight around—as it did in the early

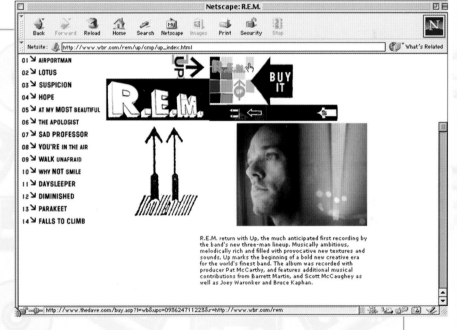

1980s when it virtually killed off the superior **DAT** cassette as a domestic format. The Internet, however, was too global and uncontrollable to be contained. As a result, the music industry has reluctantly had to accept that in the future downloading and purchasing from the Internet are certain to play an increasingly important role in both the marketing and selling of music.

Evidence of this change in attitude can be seen in the way that the major entertainment corporations, who own much of the music industry, have begun to forge business links or mergers with some of the major Internet service providers.

**Above: Warner's website for R.E.M.'s album *Up*, seen here, contained information on the album and the group. The website also gave the user the option to buy the CD.**

# CHAPTER 5

# The Recording Process

The process of recording a cassette, CD, or record begins in a recording studio and finishes in a factory. A variety of technicians and equipment will be needed along the way, from recording the first sounds to manufacturing the final product.

Most of the music that people hear on TV and radio or buy in a record store was originally created in a recording studio. Recording studios can range from rather small recording systems that cost less than a few hundred dollars and can be set up in the home, to multimillion-dollar state-of-the-art **professional** systems, some of which can cost thousands of dollars a day to rent.

### The recording studio

A typical professional recording studio consists of two separate zones: the control room and the "live" room. The live room is the place where the musicians set up their equipment and play. The microphones and other sound sources are set up in this room and connected by cables to the recording equipment in the adjoining control room. Ideally, the two rooms

**Above: A control room of London's Whitfield Street Recording Studios. Above the mixing console (bottom) are a computer for hard-disk recording, two sets of loudspeakers, and the window to the live room.**

should be sufficiently soundproofed so that the noise created by the musicians can only be heard through the loudspeakers in the control room.

The control room is where the technicians—the producer and engineer responsible for recording the session—are located. At its most basic the control room will contain a mixing console to balance the sound levels, recording equipment, various types of loudspeakers, and electronic effects to alter the sounds.

Low-cost studios, serving musicians who are **semiprofessional** or those on a low **budget**, are often one-person businesses—with the owner taking on all of the different jobs, from booking recording sessions to producing the finished work. In the larger studios these tasks are usually assigned to various different individuals.

### The tape operator

Starting at the bottom of the ranks, the tape operator (sometimes called the assistant engineer) is the most junior member of the studio team. Although the job title suggests that

---

*A tape operator job is the standard way to enter the world of studio recording*

---

operating the recording equipment is the main task, in practice he or she is more likely to be a kind of studio gofer—someone who does the things that nobody else wants to do. Typical jobs will include the maintaining and cleaning of equipment, making cups of coffee, and fetching whatever the engineer or musicians need.

Taking a job as a tape operator (or "tape op" as it is often abbreviated) is a standard way of entering the world

of professional recording. Since the job is generally low-paid, it is usually aimed at candidates in their teens or early twenties. Such positions are not generally advertised and are often filled by those "in the know" or who have connections in or with the studio, yet some studios might keep someone's name on file if they were impressed by their approach or their previous experience. Qualifications on paper are not likely to cut too much ice in this area; more important is the ability to learn quickly, fit in with other members of the team, and show a willingness to do whatever is asked.

Although that may not sound like a whole lot of fun, there are many advantages to be had as a studio "insider." The tape operator gets to

**Above: A tape operator at Swan Yard Recording Studios in London is putting what is called a "two-inch reel-to-reel tape" on a multitrack recorder. Although the process of recording has become increasingly digital, bypassing the need for reel-to-reel tape and tape recorders, some artists still prefer to record on reel-to-reel, and many recording studios still offer this equipment.**

meet a wide array of music business figures, from musicians to record-label bosses; and this development of new contacts and **"networking"** are crucial to a career in the music world. Furthermore, many tape ops are given free access to the studios during downtime—periods in which the studio is not being rented—and this offers an opportunity to put what has been learned into practice. The job may appear to be extremely menial—that is, requiring much activity and not a great deal of thought—but many top engineers and producers have graduated from this position.

## The engineer

The responsibility for getting the musicians' sound recorded in the best possible way belongs to the engineer. A good engineer is able to select, set up, and operate all the recording equipment according to the artists' needs. This involves a complete understanding of microphone technique, including the specific models of microphone that are best suited to an instrument or voice, and the ability to get the best out of the mixing console and racks of electronic effects. Engineers are also responsible for engineering the final **mix** and preparing the music for **CD** or **record** manufacture. Many engineers also have ambitions to become producers and will sometimes function as such in the absence of any designated producer or any clear idea for the sound from the musicians involved. A skillful engineer who understands and empathizes with what the artist is trying to achieve is an enormous benefit to a recording session.

Engineers usually work for a studio or are self-employed **freelancers**. Many will also have graduated from being tape ops, although studios that specialize in classical recordings often favor so-called "tonmeister" engineers—those who have studied sound recording and **acoustics** to a high level in college or university.

Like all members of the studio team, however, there is more to doing the job successfully than just having the necessary skills. Making music is a creative process, and the engineer will

**Below: An engineer setting the volume levels on the mixing console. An engineer will often use a pad of paper (right) to write down specific instructions received from the artists or any technical details that must be remembered.**

play an important role in helping create the right "vibe" for the session to go smoothly. It is probably fair to say that people who have "difficult" or unreceptive personalities are not likely to thrive as recording engineers in the long run.

## The producer

The producer is the manager of the recording session. He or she will ultimately seek to help the artists achieve the results they are looking for, with an understanding of exactly what needs to be done, where it has to be done, and by whom it should be done. A good producer will have contacts and knowledge of the best studios available. Some will even maintain a team of engineers they prefer to work with. Perhaps the most important of the producer's tasks is to take on the role of the objective voice

of the recording session, stepping back when necessary, and not being afraid to tell artists what is and isn't working, whether it be their sound, playing, or the musical **arrangement**.

Approaches to running a recording session vary greatly. Some producers will take an extremely "hands-on" approach, supervising or even taking over the engineering tasks. At the other end of the scale other producers simply turn up at the end of the session to oversee the final mix.

The most famous producers are usually self-employed. In many cases they earn as much money as the artists they work with—especially when they are able to demand a percentage of the sales **royalties**. Others are employed by record labels or the recording studios themselves. Many producers graduated from engineer status, although it is also

**Above: Legendary producer and arranger Quincy Jones (right) goes over an arrangement with hip-hop singer and songwriter Big Daddy Kane. Jones has worked with many of the world's most successful musicians, including jazz stars like Miles Davis and Thelonius Monk, solo singers like Frank Sinatra and Aretha Franklin, and dance-music superstars like Michael Jackson and Will Smith.**

# THE MAN BEHIND THE BEATLES' SOUND

In some cases the producer's role is so important that they end up becoming an essential part of a band's sound. A case in point is that of George Martin (b. 1926), the man who during the 1960s produced all of the Beatles' recordings—a catalog that includes some of the best-known songs and albums in the history of pop music.

Martin studied at London's Guildhall School of Music before eventually taking a job with EMI's Parlophone label. His responsibilities included producing recording sessions and scouting for new talent. Before he discovered the Beatles, his label was better known for producing British comedy acts.

When the Beatles first began recording with Martin, they would play their songs to him on **acoustic** guitars. He would make suggestions for how the parts should be arranged for the whole band. His influence increased as the Beatles' music became more ambitious. By understanding the ideas that they wanted to bring to their music, Martin was able to use his classical training to introduce elements of which the musicians had little experience or exposure. This can be heard in the sophisticated string arrangements on songs like "Yesterday" and "Eleanor Rigby." Equally, Martin's mastery of studio techniques saw the creation of recordings like "Strawberry Fields Forever"—widely regarded as the greatest single ever made.

The relationship between band and producer peaked with the album *Sgt. Pepper's Lonely Hearts Club Band*. By this time the level of public recognition of Martin's influence on the band was so great that one of the Beatles, Paul McCartney, began to take exception to the amount of media attention being lavished on his producer.

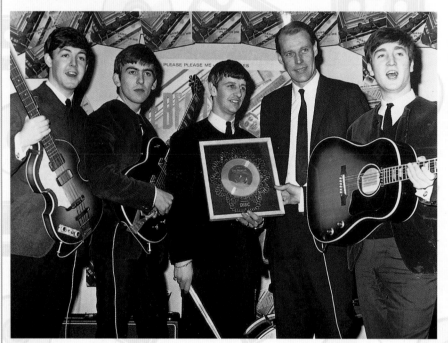

**Above: John Lennon (right) of the Beatles displays one of the band's many hit records produced by George Martin (second from right).**

quite common for musicians with a great deal of studio experience to make such a career move.

Some producers take their job even farther and develop their own artistic and commercial visions. This may include scouting for talent, managing the artists they discover, recording the music, and negotiating record deals. Many of the producers of the popular young "boy bands" of the past decade operate in this way: Although some of these singers have become famous pop stars, they are often just salaried employees on the producer's payroll.

**Remix producers**

New technology and the popularity of dance music have changed many aspects of studio life in recent years. The use of computer **sequencers** and **hard-disk recording** systems has seen the emergence of a new generation of producers referred to as "remix producers." They may be called on to rebuild an existing song from scratch, perhaps with only a vocal part from which to work. Remixers tend to fall into two categories: they are either musicians who are experienced with making music on computers or club

DJs who may know little or nothing about recording techniques or musicianship, but have a finger firmly on the pulse of what young, cutting-edge audiences want to buy.

## Preparing for the studio

Those artists who have their own recording facilities (or an unlimited recording budget) can afford to make the studio their everyday working environment: they can write, arrange, and rehearse the material just before or at the same time as they record. Yet this can be an expensive luxury, and in most cases certain stages of preparation are planned out carefully before an artist goes into the studio in order to keep studio costs down.

For most modern-day recording artists the first stage in this process is to compose the songs and select the ones most suitable for recording. The music formats sold in stores often influence this process—for example, a CD album usually lasts somewhere between 45 and 70 minutes. Most artists therefore choose songs that will create the right mood or impression when played in sequence, or those that have hooks—memorable tunes, lyrics, or catchy **choruses**—and are more likely to get played on the radio or noticed in reviews.

The next stage is to make quick, cheap, and fairly rough recordings known as "**demos**" (taken from the word "demonstration"). With the development of inexpensive, easy-to-use home recording equipment, many songwriters create their demos in their own homes. On the simplest level a demo can be little more than singing over a simple acoustic guitar backing. In fact, this approach is often a favored starting point. Even if the

*Below: Top British DJ Pete Tong (b. 1960) mixing at a London club. Tong's series of* Essential Selection *CDs, the first of which was released in 1997, are among the world's best-selling remix albums.*

**Above:** This live room at the Abbey Road Recording Studio in London, seen through the window of the control room, is large enough to contain an entire orchestra. It is therefore a popular place for symphony orchestras to record.

eventual finished song will have a full band backing it and elaborate orchestral parts added to it, hearing the song in its most basic form is a good way of evaluating its quality.

The final stage—rehearsing—is extremely important. It is the time for experimenting with different musical arrangements; it is also when most of the basic problems should be ironed out, such as finding the correct **tempo** or playing the song in a **key** that suits the vocalist's **range**. Most important of all, rehearsals allow a band to lock into its own **groove**, creating a "tight" feel or strong sense of togetherness—essential for the creation of great music.

Rehearsals can be held in any place where loud music noise can be played without bothering the outside world. Most bigger towns or cities have soundproofed rehearsal studios that can be rented by the hour.

Before recording an album it is advantageous to have more material ready—that is, written, arranged, and rehearsed—than might appear to be needed. This allows for unforeseen future problems, since sometimes even the best songs just don't "work" when recorded in a certain way.

## Choosing a studio

There are two major considerations when choosing a studio: the cost and the facilities. These two factors often go hand in hand. Traditionally, studios tended to set their charges according to the number of **tracks** their tape machines were capable of recording; and when advertising, they tended to define themselves in this way—for example, "an eight-track studio" or "a 24-track studio." Nowadays matters are less clear-cut, since even low-budget computer recording makes it possible for home users to record up to 48 tracks, or "channels," of sound. At the top end of the scale studios are more likely to charge higher rates based on the quality of their equipment, such as mixing consoles and electronic effects, and their downtime quarters.

The surrounding environment in which the recording takes place can also have a major influence on its successful outcome. The process of recording is usually a high-pressure situation, so top-end studios go out of their way to provide the musicians with a working environment that is as pleasant as possible. At this level the quality of the equipment in the studio and expertise of its staff are generally taken for granted, so the decision as to where to record is often made for other reasons. Some of the most expensive studios in the world provide their clients with the same sort of facilities that would be expected in a five-star hotel.

## Recording became more complex when stereo sound appeared in the 1950s

Since many studios are geared up to produce pop and rock music, the live rooms are often designed for small ensembles. Therefore, if the recording requires an orchestra or large band, it would be necessary to find a studio with a suitably large live room. Many producers favor certain studios for their ability to create specific sounds and may choose one studio to record in for its acoustics and space, and another to mix in because of its range of electronic effects equipment. In fact, it is not uncommon for a band to lay down backing tracks in one studio, add orchestral elements in a second studio, and produce the finished mixes in a third.

## The development of recording

When tape recorders were first invented, making a sound recording was a straightforward process. A microphone was put in front of the band, the tape recorder was switched on, and the band was told to start playing. If they were happy with their performance, their job was complete; if not, they played the song all over again. Much of this simplicity was due to the fact that the **hi-fi** equipment of the time was only monophonic, which means that all of the sound came out of a single loudspeaker.

This gradually changed during the 1950s when stereophonic, or stereo,

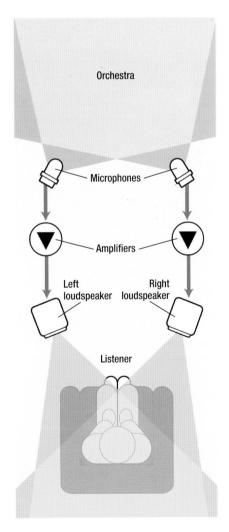

Left: A diagram showing the basic process of recording a live orchestra in stereo. Microphones are placed on either side of the orchestra in the live room to "catch" the sound. The sound is then transmitted through amplifiers and played through stereo loudspeakers. The sound recorded by each microphone is therefore "panned" through the left or right loudspeaker so that the listener hears the orchestra's music in stereo.

sound appeared, in which the sound came out of two loudspeakers. To create stereophonic sound, both the recording and playback equipment had to be equipped with a second sound channel; one was connected to the left-hand speaker, the other to the right. The sounds could then be "panned," or positioned, between the two speakers. This was made possible by feeding different amounts of volume into each speaker.

For instance, the rhythm guitar could be panned to the left, making it louder in the left loudspeaker, while the lead guitar was panned to the right, making it louder in the right loudspeaker. This separated the sound of the two guitar parts so that each one could be heard more clearly and distinctly. The birth of stereo allowed people to experience the same sort of effect in their homes as hearing music played live in a concert hall.

## Tape recorders

The 1950s also saw the birth of multitrack tape recorders—machines on which more than just two stereo tracks, or channels, could be recorded. It came about for two reasons. First, it allowed each of the instruments to be recorded on its own individual channel. This meant that the volume levels and sounds of each of the instruments could then be altered after the performance had taken place.

A second use for multitrack tape recorders is to allow a performance to be built up gradually by **overdubbing** the instruments. For example, if a tape machine has 16 different tracks, it is possible to use five tracks to record the drum set on channels one through five (see diagram below).

**Above: This state-of-the-art Alesis ADAT was the most successful digital multitrack tape recorder in the world at the beginning of the year 2000.**

**Multitrack Recording**

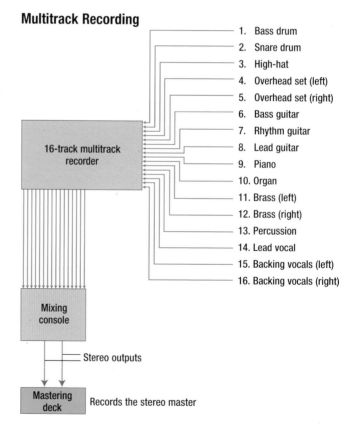

1. Bass drum
2. Snare drum
3. High-hat
4. Overhead set (left)
5. Overhead set (right)
6. Bass guitar
7. Rhythm guitar
8. Lead guitar
9. Piano
10. Organ
11. Brass (left)
12. Brass (right)
13. Percussion
14. Lead vocal
15. Backing vocals (left)
16. Backing vocals (right)

16-track multitrack recorder

Mixing console

Stereo outputs

Mastering deck — Records the stereo master

**Above: The sounds of instruments can be recorded separately on each of these 16 tracks using a multitrack tape recorder. Each track is then fed into the mixing console, and the sounds are combined for the final mix, which is recorded in stereo on the mastering deck.**

After the drummer has finished playing, the bass player can then record onto channel six while listening to the drums being played back from the first five channels. Then the rhythm guitarist can record onto channel seven while listening to the bass and drum parts, and so on. The remaining nine channels can be used in a similar way, with each musician playing along with the music on the previous channels. Often the vocals are recorded on the last channel or channels.

One advantage of working in this way is that it allows mistakes to be corrected without having to make all the musicians play their parts from scratch; another is that it allows a single musician to play several parts on the same song.

During the 1960s four- and eight-track tape recorders had become commonplace, but by the end of the 1970s most professional studios were equipped with 24-channel machines. Yet the fundamental principles on which tape recorders worked had remained the same for almost half a century—even if the sound quality had improved beyond measure.

Then, during the 1980s **digital recording** arrived, creating a cleaner, noise-free sound. Over the next 15 years traditional tape recorders quickly found themselves replaced by digital alternatives. In an increasing number of situations computers were also used to record sound, which was stored on the **hard-disk drives**. In practice, however, the principle of multitracking and overdubbing sound remains the same whichever recording system is used.

## The mixing console

Whatever the differences in sound quality or sophistication of equipment, the basic principles of modern recording are the same. The performance is captured on a multitrack tape recorder; then the multitrack channels are "mixed down" and recorded onto a two-channel stereo "mastering" tape, which becomes the finished article.

**Below: The AMS Neve DFC digital film mixing console, showing the faders and dials that are used to adjust the volume, panning, and other aspects of the sound in a recording.**

These two processes both require the use of a mixing console.

The mixing console—also known as "the console," "the mixing board," or simply the "board"—is the very heart of every recording studio. There are two distinct ways in which it is used: first, as a way of getting the original sounds of the performer onto the multitrack recorder; second, to "mix" the multitrack channels down into a finished stereo recording. The mixing console is like a giant switchboard in which signals are connected to a series of input channels, altered by various effects, and rerouted to a series of output channels (see diagram on page 63).

For recording onto a multitrack machine—whether **analog** or digital tape or computer hard disk—the microphones and instruments are connected to the input channels of the mixing console. These signals are then routed into the various channels of the multitrack recorder.

For the "**mixdown**" of the music each channel of the multitrack is plugged into one of the console's input channels. Each sound on the multitrack can then be altered or panned differently between the two loudspeakers. All of the channels are played at the same time to produce a "balanced" sound. When all involved in the mixdown are happy with the balance of sounds, the final mix is recorded onto the stereo mastering recorder, connected to two output signals leaving the mixing console.

## Sound effects

Not only can a sound that has already been recorded be altered by changing the EQ on the mixing console, but more dramatic alterations can be

**Right:** Pianos can produce a lot of sound reverberation or boom when they are played. Although a certain amount of reverberation can enhance the sound quality, too much can interfere with the purity of the sound. Therefore, many recording studios use special acoustic tiles on the walls and ceiling to absorb any excess reverberation.

# THE MAIN INPUT CHANNELS ON A MIXING CONSOLE

The input channels of the mixing console are identical in that they all feature a variety of different functions for altering the sound.

1. Equalization (**EQ**): These are the **tone** controls. They are rather like an extended version of the bass and treble controls on a hi-fi system. They alter the sound by splitting it into different **frequencies**, each of which can then be cut or boosted in volume.
2. Pan: This controls where the sound will be positioned between the two loudspeakers. If the controls are turned as far as possible in either direction, all the sound will only come from one of the speakers.
3. Volume fader: This "slider" controls the overall volume of the sound on that channel. The higher it is pushed, the more the volume of sound recorded on that channel is boosted.

### Functions of the Mixing Console

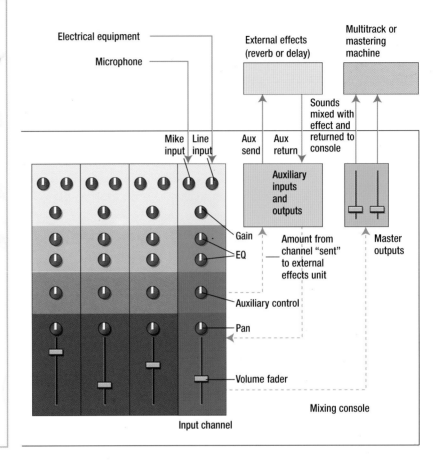

created by using special electronic sound effects. The two most common types are reverb and delay.

## Reverb

Reverberation is a natural acoustic phenomenon. Adding electronic reverberation (usually known simply as "reverb") creates the effect of the sound spreading out. It is similar to the sound one hears when walking into a tunnel or entering a room that has no carpets, curtains, or furniture. After each step one hears not only the sound of one's foot hitting the floor but an aftereffect caused by the sound bouncing off the walls and ceiling.

Some instruments are recorded so that the natural reverberation is also captured, yet it is also common to record instruments like the drums or the human voice in as "dry" a fashion

as possible. That is why some live rooms are heavily padded, so that the sound is absorbed by the walls and doesn't bounce back into the room (see photograph at left).

Artificial reverb is created using a special piece of digital equipment. The advantage of adding this effect to a dry signal during the mixdown is that it is possible to program specific reverb sounds, thereby re-creating the effect of adding reverberation from different types of rooms. For example, a large hall with high ceilings will create a much "bigger" reverberation than a tiny room.

## Delay

A number of popular effects are also created by taking a sound and replaying it with a slight delay. At its most dramatic this takes the form of

**Above: A diagram showing the role of the mixing console in recording music. The sounds of the voices and instruments enter the mixing console through cables attached to electronic equipment or microphones. EQ, pans, volume, and auxiliary effects such as reverb and delay are then used to adjust or alter the sounds before they are mixed together and recorded on the mastering machine as the final mix.**

# RECORDING ON COMPUTER

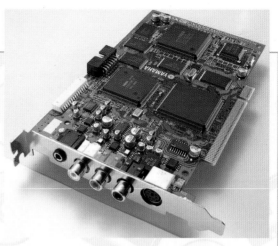

**Above: The Yamaha SW1000XG sound card.**

The pace at which new technology is developing has accelerated dramatically in recent years. The most important new development—one that is increasingly influencing the way in which recordings are made—has been the rise of computer hard-disk recording. While skills like microphone technique and mixing remain as important as ever, hard-disk recording offers composers, musicians, and producers amazing flexibility in the way in which they can create or alter sounds.

To use a computer for recording, it must be equipped with special **software**. Also, a "sound card" has to be put in to allow sound to be recorded and then played back (see photograph at right). Although there are many different recording programs, they usually appear on the computer screen with the same controls as a traditional tape recorder. Once recorded, the music can be viewed on the screen as sound

**Above: The computer screen of the Cubase program—one of the most popular programs used for hard-disk recording.**

waves, which can be edited in a variety of ways. Just as text can be "copied," "cut," and "pasted" in word-processing software, the same can be done with sound waves on the screen.

One of the most dramatic uses of this approach to recording is to alter a song's structure. Since sound waves can be viewed at the same time as all the individual tracks that make up the song (see photograph at left), it becomes possible to select one segment—a chorus, for example—and move it to a different position in the song.

The most sophisticated recording programs can reasonably claim to be nothing less than a "studio in a box," since they include not only the multitrack recorder element but also the mixer and digital effects. On the screen the image imitates that of a mixing console, showing the various tracks and what is recorded on them. The controls are moved by manipulating the computer **mouse**.

an echo. Yet if a signal with a delay of less than 35 milliseconds is mixed in with the original sound, instead of a complete echo a variety of swirling effects like **phasing** and **flanging** are created. Although they are "natural" acoustic phenomena, these effects are created in the studio by a piece of equipment called a digital delay unit.

## Using electronic effects

Like the mixing console, reverb and delay units have input and output connections. The original signal is connected to the unit's input socket,

and the altered signal comes out of the unit's output socket. Although it would be possible to take every output from a multitrack recorder and connect each one to its own unique reverb or delay unit, mixing consoles have a feature that allows for varying amounts of each signal to pass into one unit. It is called the "auxiliary" control (see diagram on page 63).

The mixing console has both "send" and "return" connections for each auxiliary. The send connection is linked to the input socket, and the return is linked to the output socket of the effect unit. Each input channel of the mixing console is equipped with at least one auxiliary control. Rotating this control dial determines the volume of the sound that is sent through and returned from the effects unit and therefore how much of the effect is added.

## The finished product

Once a recording has been mixed down to a stereo master, it is almost ready for mass production. There are five major formats on which recorded music is bought—compact disk (CD), vinyl record, **cassette**, **minidisk**, and MP3 (see box on page 67). CD is the most commercially important format, although records remain popular in specialized markets, such as the dance "12-inch." Cassette and minidisk are mainly used for home taping. Artists signed to major labels may have their music available on all these formats. The high costs involved, however, mean that independent musicians are apt to release their work on CD only.

Whatever the format, the process of manufacturing involves a number of stages, the first of which is always postproduction mastering (sometimes also known as "the cut"—a hangover from the days of vinyl records).

## Making records

The process for producing a vinyl record begins in a small specialized studio called the mastering suite. The original master tape is played back through a mixing console that is linked to a lathe—a machine that cuts a groove into a blank lacquer (a type of varnish like shellac) disk while it is being rotated. This is "the cut." Last-minute changes, such as altering the volumes and EQs or fading out songs, can still be made while the master

Below: Stampers in a record-making plant are used to press the molten vinyl into a record. One stamper is used to press the A-side of the record, while the other stamper is used for the B-side.

tape is being transferred to the lacquer. This work is done by a mastering engineer.

The lacquer is then sent off for "plating," where it is coated with a thin layer of silver and electroplated in a nickel solution. When the plating is stripped away, it holds a negative impression of the original lacquer. This is used to make the "stamper"—one stamper is needed for each side of the record. For the pressing, molten vinyl is compressed hydraulically between the two stampers, creating the finished record.

## CD production

In spite of the amazing technology involved, producing a compact disk is a relatively fast and straightforward process. The postproduction work also takes place in what is called a mastering suite. The original stereo recording is "remastered," and special codes are added that provide the CD with the information it needs to function properly, such as track numbers, index points, start times, and durations of the songs.

The recorded information is transferred physically to the disk by way of a recording laser. To do this, the environment of the mastering suite must be entirely free of dust and vibrations, since they can interfere with the focus of the recording laser, which must be exact. As well as transmitting information to the disk, the laser adjusts the disk's spin rate, which can be between 200 and 500 revolutions per second. The disk is then dipped into an etching chemical that burns away all the areas that have been exposed to the laser, cutting tiny pits of varying depths into the disk's light-sensitive material. This results in a master CD, called a "glass master," from which the CDs are duplicated.

**Below: A factory worker inspects the "glass master" for a CD before creating the duplicate CDs that will be sold to the public.**

The pressing of CDs is similar to the pressing of a vinyl record. The CD is electroplated in the pressing plant to produce "stampers," from which the CD is then mass produced.

The molded plastic of each CD is exposed to vaporized aluminum or silver and sealed in acrylic before it is packaged and ready to be sold as the final product to the consumer.

**Above: CDs being mass produced in the Philips factory.**

## MP3 AND THE INTERNET

Over the past decade the Internet has changed the whole nature of communications, so it comes as no surprise to find that it has also begun to make an important impression on the music business. Musicians were quick to see the potential of the Web for promoting their activities. Many began to make snatches of their music available to the public for **downloading**. Yet the problem with this approach was that downloading large sound-files was a very time-consuming process, and the sound quality was often not very good.

The answer to this problem came in the development of MP3.

MP3 is a computer file format that allows CD-quality music to be compressed and downloaded quickly from a website onto a home computer. The MP3 format is especially attractive to independent or unsigned musicians in that their music can be distributed without the costs and risks associated with the manufacturing of a CD. Many people believe that more and more music will be bought and sold in this way in the near future.

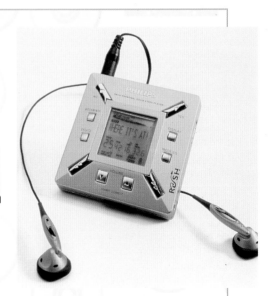

**Above: A Philips MP3 Player.**

# TIMELINE

**c.41,000 B.C.** Musical instruments like flutes are made out of bones, shells, and sticks.

**c.10,000 B.C.** Andean peoples in South America begin playing wind and percussion instruments.

**c.3000 B.C.** Egyptians write songs and play flutes, harps, trumpets, tambourines, and drums.

**c.2000 B.C.** Pentatonic (five-note) scale is developed.

**c.1400 B.C.** The Chinese play drums, bells, flutes, and chimes.

**c.1100 B.C.** The Chinese are using the zither and a mouth organ called the *sheng*.

**c.550 B.C.** Greek philosopher Pythagoras originates the idea of notes, octaves, pitches, and scales.

**c.380 B.C.** Greek philosophers encourage music education. Instruments include the *kithara* (a lyre) and *aulos* (like an oboe).

**c.350 B.C.** Greek theorist Aristoxenus identifies rhythm, semitones, and explains scales.

**c.300 B.C.** Greek engineer Ktesibios invents the organ, using water to control the air pressure.

**c.100 A.D.** Christians sing hymns and psalms, using a solo-and-response method.

**late 500s A.D.** Pope Gregory I standardizes church music, known as Gregorian chant, or plainsong.

**700s A.D.** Moors invade Spain and southern Europe, bringing their instruments, sliding modes, and the origins of flamenco.

**c.800 A.D.** The Japanese classical music known as *gagaku* begins.

**800s A.D.** Air pumped through bellows replaces water as the means for working an organ.

**900s A.D.** Bowed instruments are brought to Europe from Asia.

**c.1025** Guido d'Arezzo invents musical notation, including staves.

**1000s–1100s** Minstrels roam Europe performing secular music.

**1100s** Organum music leads to the more complex, multiple-part music known as polyphony.

**late 1100s** Drums become a common rhythm-keeping instrument in Europe.

**1200s** In France composers adapt plainsong to invent the motet—a form of vocal polyphonic music.

**1300s** A system of harmony develops out of plainsong in France and Italy.

**early 1300s** Persian Amir Khusrau creates Indian classical music, Sufi *qawwali* music, and the sitar.

**1400s** The slide trombone is developed.

**1476** The first music books of plainsong are printed.

**c.1500** Muslims invade Indonesia and note that gamelan music has been around for centuries.

**1500s** The French chanson (song) becomes popular—it often told a story of lost love.

Italian musicians begin writing original music and introduce dynamics and orchestration.

In England Thomas Tallis writes many anthems, which become an important musical form.

In the Lutheran church the congregation joins in the singing, and hymns are in the local language (rather than Latin).

**1501** Ottaviano dei Petrucci publishes the first book of polyphonic music.

**c.1550s** The first *son* song is performed in Santiago, Chile.

**1558** Italian composer Gioseffo Zarlino publishes *Le istitutioni harmoniche*, which describes the use of chords in writing harmony.

**late 1500s** Music appears with specific parts for female singers.

Nicola Vincentino begins writing madrigals—songs for several unaccompanied voices.

**1594** Jacopo Peri composes *Dafne*, the first opera.

**1597** English composer John Dowland publishes four books of songs with lute accompaniment.

**1600** Dawn of the Baroque era.

**1600s** African slaves are brought to Europe and America, bringing their music with them.

Oratorios start to develop at religious meetings held by the Italian Filippo Neri.

Castrati are singing in operas.

**1620** Pilgrims arrive in America from Europe bringing their psalms and hymns with them.

**1685** Johann Sebastian Bach born in Germany.

**1689** The English opera *Dido and Aeneas* by Henry Purcell opens in London.

**early 1700s** Johann Christoff Denner invents the clarinet.

**1709** Bartolomeo Cristofori invents the pianoforte (the piano).

**1722** Bach publishes *The Well-tempered Clavichord*, a collection of keyboard pieces in all the major and minor keys.

**1727** The first German singspiel (*The Devil Is Loose*) is produced.

**1731** The first formal classical concert takes place in America.

**1742** The first performance of Handel's oratorio *Messiah*.

**1748** The first public concert hall opens in Oxford, England.

**c.1750** The Classical era begins.

**1756** Wolfgang Amadeus Mozart born in Salzburg, Austria.

**1770** William Billings publishes the first book of American music, *The New-England Psalm-Singer*.

Ludwig van Beethoven born in Bonn, Germany.

**1777** "Yankee Doodle" is the first American song published in Europe.

**1786** Mozart composes his opera *The Marriage of Figaro*.

**late 1700s** German composers start writing lieder, songs in which the lyrics are all-important.

**1790** The first performance of Peking (Beijing) opera.

**1791–1795** "Father of the symphony" Joseph Haydn writes his 12 "London" symphonies, including his *Surprise* Symphony.

**c.1800** Beethoven increases the size of the classical orchestra and ushers in the Romantic era.

The waltz grows in popularity throughout Europe.

**1800s** African-American slaves use Christian hymns as the basis for their own spirituals.

**early 1800s** Caribbean and African styles combine in Sierra Leone to create "highlife."

**1814** "The Star-Spangled Banner" is first performed.

**1823** Beethoven completes his Ninth Symphony.

**mid-1840s** Blackfaced minstrel shows become popular in America and Britain.

**1853** First performance of Verdi's opera *La Traviata*.

**c.1850s** The banjo becomes a popular instrument among gold miners in America.

European composers start writing nationalistic music.

**c.1860** Vienna, Austria, becomes the main center of operetta.

**1864** Adolphe Sax invents the saxophone.

**1871** Spirituals are first performed for a white audience by the Jubilee Singers.

**1876** Brahms completes his First Symphony.

First performance of Wagner's four-opera cycle *The Ring of the Nibelungen*.

**1877** First performance of Tchaikovsky's ballet *Swan Lake*.

**1878** David Edward Hughes invents the carbon microphone.

**1879** Bandleader Miguel Failde creates *danzón* dance music.

**late 1800s** Appalachian folk music is adapted into hillbilly—and later country—music.

Barbershop quartet singing becomes popular in America.

Millions of copies of sheet music are sold for people to play songs on their pianos at home.

African Americans start performing the blues.

**c.1890** Vaudeville becomes America's most popular form of mass entertainment.

**1891** Carnegie Hall opens in New York City.

**1894** First performance of the impressionist *Prélude à l'après-midi d'un faune* by Debussy.

Emil Berliner invents the gramophone and the record disk.

**1896** First performance of Puccini's opera *La Bohème*.

**1899** Scott Joplin's "Maple Leaf Rag" helps make ragtime popular.

**c.1900** Expressionist composers begin placing equal importance on all 12 semitones of the scale.

Mariachi bands begin performing in Mexico.

**early 1900s** In New Orleans African-American marching bands form the first jazz groups.

African Americans adapt "shout" songs and church "witness" rituals to make gospel.

Austrian composers Arnold Schoenberg and Alban Berg develop *Sprechgesang* singing.

**1901** Premiere of Rachmaninov's Second Piano Concerto.

**1902** Enrico Caruso makes recordings for the gramophone.

**1906** Béla Bartók begins recording Hungarian folk songs.

**1909** William Ludwig invents the foot pedal for the bass drum.

**c.1910** Tin Pan Alley starts producing popular songs.

**1911** Premiere of Richard Strauss's opera *Der Rosenkavalier.*

**1913** First performance in Paris of Stravinsky's *The Rite of Spring* causes a riot in the audience.

**1917** The Original Dixieland Jazz Band makes the first phonograph recordings of jazz tunes.

**1920** Léon Thérémin invents the "theremin," the first important electronic instrument.

Mamie Smith's "Crazy Blues" is the first blues recording featuring a black performer.

**1920–1923** Arnold Schoenberg writes his first pieces of serialist music, based on a tone row.

**1920s** The jazz age. Chicago replaces New Orleans as the center of jazz.

The first jug bands are formed.

The beginnings of electronic music.

*Enka*, combining Western music with traditional Japanese minor modes, develops in Japan.

Blues guitarists develop the slide technique of gliding the fingers up and down the strings instead of using the frets.

The amplifier is invented.

The tango becomes popular in America and Europe.

Dance-band singers start using the microphone.

Blues musicians start playing a "walking bass," which leads to boogie-woogie.

Muzak begins recording production (background) music.

Sheet-music sales decrease as record sales increase.

**1921** Prokofiev's opera *The Love for Three Oranges* first performed.

**1923** King Oliver's Creole Jazz Band, featuring Louis Armstrong on trumpet, makes the first jazz

recordings by an all-black group.

The first country record, Fiddlin' John Carson's "The Little Old Log Cabin in the Lane," is made in Atlanta, Georgia.

**1924** Premiere of George Gershwin's *Rhapsody in Blue.*

**1925** George Dewey Hay begins broadcasting a radio show—later known as *The Grand Ole Opry*—from Nashville, Tennessee.

**1926** Louis Armstrong invents "scat singing."

**1927** Premiere of the first modern musical—Jerome Kern and Oscar Hammerstein II's *Show Boat.*

The first motion picture with sound is *The Jazz Singer.*

**1928** Joe Falcon's "Allons a Lafayette" is the first Cajun record.

Kurt Weill and Bertolt Brecht's musical *The Threepenny Opera* includes political satire.

**1930s** "Swing"—African-American dance music—becomes popular.

Folk singer Woody Guthrie sings songs about the Depression.

**1934** The Hammond organ is invented by Laurens Hammond.

Magnetic recording tape is developed.

**1935** The electric guitar and the tape recorder are invented.

**1938** Mambo music begins in Cuba.

**1940s** Latin music begins to influence American jazz.

Big-band singers Ella Fitzgerald, Peggy Lee, and Frank Sinatra embark on solo careers.

Bebop emerges as improvisational jazz music.

**1943–1959** Rodgers and Hammerstein write a string of successful musicals.

**1944** Premiere of Aaron Copland's ballet *Appalachian Spring.*

**late 1940s** Dance "race music" becomes "rhythm and blues."

*Musique concrète* is used in orchestral compositions.

The electric piano is invented.

**1948** The long-playing 33⅓ record (the LP) is introduced.

**1949** "Father of honky-tonk" Hank Williams has first big hit with "Lovesick Blues."

Miles Davis releases *Birth of the Cool*, the first "cool jazz" record.

**1950s** Leo Fender designs the Telecaster and the Stratocaster electric guitars.

A new music called bossa nova emerges from Brazil—a light jazz sound with samba and *choro* influences.

Young African Americans start singing doo-wop.

"Soul" emerges, adapted from the gospel sound.

Technological advances include tape recording and stereo.

**1951** Elliot Carter composes his atonal String Quartet No. 1.

**1952** Pierre Boulez composes his serialist piece *Structures I.*

John Cage performs his experimental piece *4' 33".*

**1953** Enrique Jorrin invents the cha-cha-cha.

**mid-1950s** DJ Alan Freed coins the term "rock 'n' roll."

**1955** The first synthesizer is built.

**1956** Elvis Presley reaches No. 1 with the rock 'n' roll song "Heartbreak Hotel."

Frank Sinatra releases *Songs for Swinging Lovers.*

**1959** Stockhausen performs his aleatory piece *Zyklus.*

Miles Davis abandons cool in favor of modal jazz.

Rock 'n' roll star Buddy Holly is killed in a place crash.

Berry Gordy and Smokey Robinson start Motown Records.

**1960** The Shirelles become the first black girl group to have a No. 1 hit single.

Saxophonist Ornette Coleman starts a new improvisational jazz sound called "free jazz."

**1960s** Period performances of Baroque pieces become popular.

The Andean music known as *chicha* is developed.

**1962** The Beatles make their first record, "Love Me Do."

**1963** "Queen of Country" Patsy Cline dies in a plane crash.

Bob Dylan records the 1960s folk anthem "Blowin' in the Wind."

**1965** James Brown introduces a new style of dance music, "funk."

Folk rock begins when Bob Dylan plays an electric guitar instead of an acoustic one at the Newport Jazz Festival.

The analog synthesizer is made available to the public.

**late 1960s** Some bands begin playing psychedelic rock.

Progressive rock emerges.

**1967** Digital recording technology is developed.

The Beatles release *Sgt. Pepper's Lonely Hearts Club Band.*

**1968** Steppenwolf's "Born to Be Wild" is first heavy metal record.

Country singer Johnny Cash releases *Live at Folsom Prison.*

**1969** Miles Davis combines free jazz and rock to form "fusion."

**1970s** Indian music becomes popular in the West.

Salsa becomes a popular type of Latin-based dance music.

Jamaica's reggae begins to spread around the world.

**mid-1970s** Disco music becomes popular.

**1976** Punk rock band the Sex Pistols sends shock waves across Britain with "Anarchy in the U.K."

**late 1970s** The DJ-led hip-hop begins among the black urban youth of America.

**1979** Ry Cooder's album *Bop till You Drop* is the first to use a digital multitrack system.

**1980s** Cajun music enjoys a national revival.

Digital recording becomes available.

The introduction of CDs transforms the music industry.

**1981** MTV begins broadcasting on cable and satellite.

**1983** MIDI (Musical Instrument Digital Interface) enables two or more electronic instruments to communicate with each other.

**1986** Ladysmith Black Mambazo from South Africa introduces Zulu a capella music to the world.

**1987** Premiere of John Adams' minimalist opera *Nixon in China.*

**1990s** Digital sampling becomes more common in pop music.

**1996** In the violent world of gangsta rap, Tupac Shakur is shot dead in Las Vegas.

**late 1990s** Hospitals and clinics begin using music therapy.

Internet users begin downloading music onto their personal computers.

# Glossary

**acoustic** The term for any instrument that is not electrically amplified.

**acoustics** The qualities of an auditorium that determine how well sound is heard in it.

**advance** A payment made "in advance" to finance work in progress, before it is completed.

**amateur** (musician) Someone who plays music purely for pleasure rather than in order to earn a living.

**analog** Circuitry that uses a continuous but varying electrical signal to record or produce sound, as opposed to **digital**, which changes electrical signals into digital information (made up of the numbers 0 and 1).

**aria** An elaborate solo song, usually forming part of an opera.

**arranger** Someone who rewrites musical compositions or adapts them for different instruments.

**budget** The amount of money assigned to or available for a particular project.

**cantata** A vocal composition in several movements for soloists and a **chorus**, accompanied by an orchestra.

**cassette** A small plastic cartridge containing two reels of magnetic tape that is used for recording sound or that already has sound recorded on it.

**CD** Short for compact disk. A metal disk covered in clear plastic, containing recorded music or computer data.

**choral** A term used to describe a piece of music designed for singing by a group of singers or **chorus**.

**choreography** The art of arranging the movements and dance steps in a ballet or other dance performance.

**chorus** An organized group of singers, usually of nonchurch music, or the section of a song that comes after the verse and is usually repeated again at the end of each verse.

**copyright** The exclusive legal right to reproduce, publish, and sell a musical or other artistic work.

**DAT (digital audio tape)** A plastic cartridge, smaller than a cassette, that contains digital recording tape for use in a DAT recorder.

**demo** An informal term for a recording used to "demonstrate" an artist's talent or a composer's music.

**digital music** Music that is produced using **digital recording**.

**digital recording** A way of recording that uses binary code (the numbers 0 and 1) to process sound information (as opposed to **analog**).

**downloading** The process of transferring data from the Internet or a computer onto another computer or storage disk like a **CD**.

**drum fill** A short sequence played on the drums that "fills" the space between musical phrases.

**EQ** Short for "equalization," which refers to the **tone** controls, such as treble and bass, on a mixing console or **hi-fi** system.

**flanging** An electronic effect that produces a "whooshing" sound.

**freelance/freelancer** People who work for themselves and are not associated with any particular employer.

**frequency** The measure of the **pitch** of a note according to the number of vibrations per second that the note gives off.

**gig** A booking for a band or artist to perform. The term is also used as another word for a concert.

**gramophone** The first type of record player that reproduced recorded sounds by means of the vibration of a stylus or needle, which followed the groove on a revolving, flat vinyl disk.

**groove** A slang term that describes the feeling of "tightness" a group or band gets when the music "comes together" during or after rehearsals.

**gross** The full amount of a sum of money before deductions are taken out.

**grunge** A mixture of heavy metal and punk that emerged in Seattle and became popular in the late 1980s.

**hard-disk drive** The main storage device on a computer.

**hard-disk recording** The recording and storing of music on the hard disk of a computer.

**hi-fi** Short for high fidelity; in the 1970s the term described the highest quality electronic sound then available.

**home page** The name for the first screen page of a website.

**improvise/improvisation** Creating music spontaneously, without planning what is going to be played or sung.

**jingles** The term for short snatches of music recorded for use in advertising.

**key** The home **scale** of a musical composition; also part of a keyboard.

**loop** A short musical recorded phrase that is often repeated during a song.

**march** A piece of music with a regular rhythm that is played by a military band to help soldiers keep in step.

**minidisk** A small disk like a mini **CD**, used as a format for recorded music. The format was developed by Sony.

**mix** To add together all the recorded tracks of a musical composition and then balance the sound.

**mixdown** The music on a tape after all the recorded tracks have been added together and the sounds have been balanced and altered to the satisfaction of the producer, artists, and engineer.

**mode** One of a series of **scales** used in medieval times and still in use in some modern forms of music, such as folk and jazz.

**mouse** A small mouse-sized plastic object attached to a computer that is used to click on various icons on the screen to instruct the computer to enter into programs.

**mute** A device used to soften or muffle the **tone color** of some acoustic instruments, like violins or trumpets.

**networking** Making social contact with people who might be helpful in furthering one's career.

**new wave** A style of music that appeared in the late 1970s that combined the raw energy of **punk rock** with a brighter pop sound.

**notation** A system of writing down music for others to learn and perform.

**overdubbing** To record a performance onto a track of tape over a previously used track, or to build up a recording by recording onto an unused track.

**phasing** A modulated electronic sound effect using delay that is similar to **flanging**, only more subtle.

**pitch** The sound quality of a note, whether high or low, that is determined by the **frequency** of the vibrations producing the note.

**plagiarism** Stealing or using someone else's ideas, words, or music, passing it off as one's own, and not giving the true creator any credit.

**plainsong** or plainchant—early Christian vocal music now usually referred to as Gregorian chant.

**plugger/plugging** Someone who works on behalf of artists, music publishers, or record companies to promote their music to radio DJs and other broadcasters.

**podium** A raised platform on which the conductor stands to conduct a band or an orchestra.

**professional** (musician) Someone who earns their living from making music.

**punk rock** A fast, aggressive form of rock music that became fashionable in the mid-1970s.

**range** The highest and lowest notes that a voice or an instrument is capable of making.

**record** A flat vinyl disk with a spiral groove that stores recorded music, which can be heard when the groove is traced by the needle, or stylus, on the revolving turntable of a record player.

**repertoire** A series of compositions that an artist, band, or orchestra is prepared to perform.

**royalties** Payments to songwriters every time their work is performed or a copy of their piece is sold.

**scale** A series of (usually) eight notes ascending or descending in alphabetical order and in specified intervals (whole-tones or half-tones).

**score** A written or printed manuscript containing the instrumental or vocal parts of a musical composition.

**semiprofessional** Someone who makes money from music but also does another day job to earn their living.

**sequencer** A device that records and plays back musical information through a synthesizer using a MIDI system. It allows complex compositions to be built up one part at a time.

**sight-reading** Playing a piece of music at first sight without previous rehearsal by reading musical notes, words, signs, and directions written down on paper.

**sight-singing** Singing a piece of music at first sight without previous rehearsal.

**software** Programs, procedures, and related documentation within a computer system (as opposed to hardware—the "hard" physical components of a computer system).

**tempo** The speed at which a musical piece is played, whether fast or slow.

**tone color** The sound quality of a voice or instrument.

**track** One of a varying number of separate sections on a recording tape that allow different musical parts or sounds to be built up one at a time.

**treble** The highest voice in a vocal composition in several parts, or the higher portion of the range of audio frequencies in a recording.

**unison** Two or more performers sounding the same note or melody.

**uploaded** Data transferred from a computer onto the Internet.

**virtuoso** A musician of exceptional technical skill.

# Musical Notation

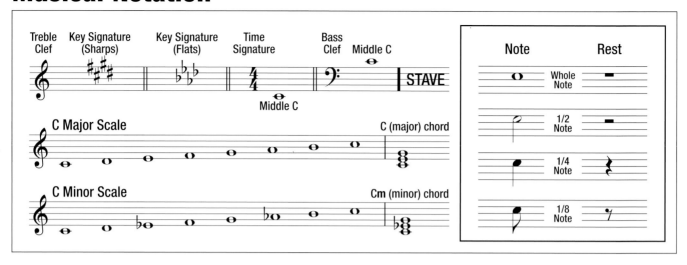

# Further Reading

Abeles, Harold F., and Charles F. Hoffer. *Foundations of Music Education*. Albany, NY: Wadsworth Publishing Company, 1994.

Bell, David A. *Getting the Best Score for Your Film: A Filmmakers' Guide to Music Scoring*. Gardena, CA: Silman-James Press, 1994.

Bentley, Nancy, and Donna W. Guthrie. *The Young Producer's Video Book: How to Write, Direct, and Shoot Your Own Video*. Brookfield, CT: Millbrook Press, 1995.

Cluck, Darrell, and Catherine S. George. *Facing the Music: Faith and Meaning in Popular Songs*. St. Louis, MO: Chalice Press, 1999.

Cutlip, Glen W., with Robert Shockley (contributor). *Careers in Teaching*. New York: Rosen Publishing Group, 1994.

Ellis, Veronica Freeman. *Wynton Marsalis* (Contemporary Biographies). Austin, TX: Raintree Steck-Vaughn, 1998.

Feinstein, Stephan. *The 1980s: From Ronald Reagan to MTV*. Berkeley Heights, NJ: Enslow Publishers, 2000.

Field, Shelly. *Career Opportunities in the Music Industry*. Mahwah, NJ: Facts on File, 2000.

Fisher, Jeffrey P. *How to Make Money: Scoring Soundtracks and Jingles*. Milwaukee, WI: Mix Books, 1997.

Freeman, John W., and Walfredo Toscanini. *Portraits of Greatness: Toscanini*. Bayside, NY: Treves Publishing Company, 1987.

Hemming, Roy (introduction). *The Melody Lingers On: The Great Songwriters and Their Movie Musicals*. New York: Newmarket Press, 1999.

Hurwitz, Johanna. *Leonard Bernstein: A Passion for Music*. Philadelphia, PA: Jewish Publication Society of America, 1993.

Lee, Barbara, and Barbara Sher. *Working in Music* (Exploring Careers). Minneapolis, MN: Lerner Publications Company, 1996.

Lutz, Norma Jean. *Marching with Sousa* (The American Adventure). Uhlrichsville, OH: Barbour & Company, 1998.

Marsh, Graham, Felix Cromey, and Glyn Callingham. *Blue Note: The Album Cover Art*. San Francisco, CA: Chronicle, 1991.

Marshall, Mary Ann. *Music: Careers in Music* (Now Hiring). Parsippany, NJ: Crestwood House, 1994.

Menuhin, Yehudi, and Sheila Schwartz. *The Violin*. New York: Abbeville Press, 1996.

Miller, Lisa Anne, and Mark Northam. *Film and Television Composer's Resource Guide: The Complete Guide to Organizing and Building Your Business*. Milwaukee, WI: Hal Leonard Publishing Corporation, 1998.

Monceaux, Morgan, and Wynton Marsalis. *Jazz; My Music, My People*. New York: A. A. Knopf, 1994.

Passman, Donald S. *All You Need to Know about the Music Business*. New York: Simon & Schuster, 1997.

Powell, Stephanie. *Hit Me with Music: How to Start, Manage, Record, and Perform with Your Own Rock Band*. Brookfield, CT: Millbrook Press, 1995.

Schalkwijk, Frans, and Andrew James (translator). *Music and People with Developmental Disabilities: Music Therapy, Remedial Music*. Philadelphia, P.A: Jessica Kingsley Publishers, 1994.

Strudwick, Leslie. *Musicians* (Women in Profile) New York: Crabtree Publishing, 1998.

Tan, Sheri. *Seiji Ozawa* (Contemporary Asian Americans). Austin, TX: Raintree Steck-Vaughn, 1997.

## Useful websites

*Blue Note Records* (contains biographies of artists who have appeared on the label)
http://www.bluenote.com

*The Cutting Edge of Music Technology* (interactive site that allows students to build their own studio)
http://edweb.fnal.gov/linc/spring96/projects_linc2/allmusic/technology/cuttingedge.html

*The Juilliard School* (official website)
http://www.juilliard.edu

*Recording Technology History* (the story of sound recording)
http://history.acusd.edu/gen/recording/notes.html

*Shinichi Suzuki Association* (overview on Suzuki's teaching methods)
http://www.suzukiassociation.org/sensei.htm

*So You Wanna Be a Rock 'n' Roll Star?* (advice for aspiring musicians)
http://www.ibslaw.com/melon/archive/202_star.html

*Want to Get Inside the Music Industry?* (tips for young people who want to work in the music business)
http://www.music-4u.com

# Set Index

Numbers in **bold type** are volume numbers.

Page numbers in *italics* refer to picture captions or a caption and text reference on the same page.